Not Mixing Up Buddhism

Essays on Women
And Buddhist Practice
Selected and Edited
by Deborah Hopkinson,
Michele Hill and Eileen Kiera,
Members of the
Kahawai Collective

WHITE PINE PRESS

ISBN 0-934834-71-7

The poem "Woman to Child" by Judith Wright is courtesy of the following: *Woman to Man* (Angus Robertson, Sydney, 1950); *Collected Poems* (Angus Robertson, Sydney, 1971) and *The Double Tree* (Houghton Mifflin, Boston).

The Diamond Sangha "Ceremony on the Death of an Unborn Child" is reprinted from *The Mind of Clover* by Robert Aitken, courtesy of North Point Press (San Francisco, 1984).

Cover illustration courtesy of Mayumi Oda.

Cover design by Barbara Pope.

Photograph by Andy Thomas.

Published by White Pine Press
76 Center Street
Fredonia, New York 14063

Not Mixing Up Buddhism

For the women of the past,
known and unknown
who have followed the path

and for our mothers and fathers,
who have shown us the way

Table of Contents

Acknowledgements

We would like to express our thanks to the contributors to this volume for their generosity in sharing their work and for the many hours they spent revising and editing their essays for publication.

Our deepest gratitude goes to Robert and Anne Aitken, who have taught us by word and by example the true meaning of Zen practice. Without them this book would not have been possible.

We are grateful to our families and friends, who supported us over the long months of meetings and deadlines as the project slowly evolved. Several people assisted as associate editors of this book: Lisa Campbell, Pamela Lee, Ann McDonald, Becky Smith, and Hannelore Stone.

We are indebted to Dennis Maloney of White Pine Press, who had total confidence in our abilities to put this book together. Thanks also to Mayumi Oda, for her beautiful cover illustration and for her ongoing support.

Finally, a very special thanks to all the people listed below who, over the years, have contributed their time, energy and talents to *Kahawai* and who have worked together to make each issue very special.

Sarah Bender
Lisa Campbell
Victoria Chau
Patricia Dougherty
Toni Hathaway
Victoria Hemphill
Kim Krull
Pamela Lee
Ann McDonald
Susan Murcott
Vicki Shook
Chris Patton
Becky Smith
Hannelore Stone
Abby Terris
Margot Wallach
Teresa Vast

The Editors,

Deborah Hopkinson
Michele Hill
Eileen Kiera

Preface

The essays collected in this volume first appeared in *Kahawai A Journal of Women and Zen*, a publication begun in 1979 as a forum and network for women in Buddhist meditation practice.

Kahawai grew out of discussions and interactions with both Buddhist and Christian women in the mid-seventies, but it was catalyzed in the fall of 1978 by two events. The first was a conference on women and religion held at Chaminade University in Honolulu where it became clear that the efforts of Jewish and Christian women to make their religious traditions more responsive were bearing fruit. At the very least, they were providing one another with a strong support system. No such network existed for women within Zen Buddhism—or any other school of Buddhism.

The second event was the arrival in Honolulu of a young woman named Susan Murcott, who joined the Diamond Sangha, a Zen Buddhist organization led by Robert Aitken, Roshi. Susan's religious search had taken her from a Boston feminist Christian group, to Japan, Australia, and finally Hawaii. I had come from the Boston area to Hawaii in 1975 to pursue a Master's degree in Asian Studies and had begun zazen practice with the Diamond Sangha soon after.

With my graduate work behind me, I would be joining Susan and ten others for a three month Zen training retreat beginning in January of 1979 at the Diamond Sangha's country center on the island of Maui. Though we had not known each other long, Susan and I both felt impelled to find a way to forge a network among women involved in Zen, as well as other Buddhist traditions, just as the Christian and Jewish women were finding ways to nurture and support one another. Coming from strong feminist backgrounds, Susan and I wanted an avenue to continue our feminist activism, and we felt that surely there must be others who, like us, were fascinated by what Dr. Rita Gross has so aptly termed, "the confluence of Buddhism and feminism."

Unlike the Judeo-Christian tradition, Zen is primarily a meditation practice rather than a set of beliefs. Although the literature of Buddhism is vast, Zen has always claimed to be "without dependence on words and scriptures."

The basic premises of the tradition are encouraging for women seeking a religious path that affirms their equality and full participation. In my graduate work I had studied the 13th century Zen master Dogen, who devoted an essay to the equality of women and decried the practice of excluding women from important Japanese religious temples. Dogen wrote, "What is more worthy about the male? Emptiness is emptiness and the five skandas (senses) are the five skandas. This is the same for male and female."

Yet while its basic teachings were of fundamental equality, and while it offered a spiritual discipline difficult to find in organized religion, Zen had spent centuries in the Confucian cultures of China and Japan and had developed as a primarily male-dominated religion. In addition, many of the teachers bringing Zen to America were Japanese themselves, and they sometimes carried with them their society's prejudicial attitudes toward women.

What would happen as this Eastern religious practice, so radical at its roots, met with the emerging feminist consciousness in the West? What effect could women have on the traditionally masculine environment and forms of ritual? What role would women play in this newly transplanted ancient path?

With Aitken Roshi's encouragement, Susan and I took our ideas to Maui, and over the next three months, *Kahawai, A Journal of Women and Zen*, was born. The training period allowed for several hours of work each day, and Susan and I devoted much of that time to planning the project. All of the other ten residents became involved. We culled names for a mailing list from old Diamond Sangha lists, restored a truly ancient mimeograph machine that Bob and Anne Aitken has used for their pioneering newsletter a decade before, and we thought, talked and wrote. Using a drawing of Kannon made by my husband, Andy Thomas, Abby Terris carved a wood block to use as our title page. Kim Krull, John Tarrant and many others helped us print the pages by hand—until the image of Kannon filled the shining floors of the meditation hall, the black ink drying in the warm air.

After much deliberation, we finally decided on a Hawaiian word, *kahawai* (ka ha wa i), meaning stream, which appeared in a poem by Aitken Roshi in his book, *A Zen Wave.*

In the kona storm
Our kahawai rages
And bufos sit deep in the mud.

Aitken Roshi's comment was: "In Hawaii, the wind blows violently from the south in a kona storm. Near the Maui Zendo, the little stream, kahawai in Hawaiian, rolls boulders and uproots trees. Big toads show only their noses." The little stream "that moves boulders and uproots trees" became our subtitle—and out statement of purpose. We hoped that through our work, and the work of other feminists, the obstacles of a patriarchal heritage within the Buddhist past would be uprooted in its move to the West.

And so we sent out the first issue—only 12 pages, without a market plan, or an audience survey, or even a clear idea if there were an audience! From the onset, *Kahawai* was a quarterly publication (we cut back to two issues a year in 1985). The first year, we produced only 200 copies, but the word soon spread, and we began sending *Kahawai*, the only journal of its kind, to over 500 people all over the world.

In the last seven years, there have been many changes—*Kahawai* volunteers have come and gone, we stopped doing the woodblocked title pages by hand long ago, and we now have new mimeograph equipment. We began by writing many of the articles ourselves, but soon women (and men) from around the country—and the world—began to send in their letters, articles and stories. Many of the contributors to *Kahawai* over the years had never published before, but they all have been overwhelmingly generous of themselves, sharing their insights and experiences in the journal's pages.

But though much has changed, the purpose has not. Rather than begin a professional publication, our hope was to stimulate discussion and sharing, as well as serve as a catalyst for change. There have been articles on many topics, including childbirth, nonviolent activism, abortion, relationships, right livelihood, lesbian women and gay men, among others. *Kahawai*'s focus has remained on Zen, because that is what we knew best, but we have often included articles by men and women practicing in other Buddhist traditions.

As of this writing, *Kahawai* continues to be produced by a handful of volunteers. Some, like Michele Hill and myself, have been with the project for years, others are brand new. But increasingly, the pressures of work and growing families are making it difficult to find time for the work.

This book is a representative collection of the work that has been done by many people on feminism and Buddhism. It is not an introduction to Zen as such, but will hopefully spark interest in Zen practice, especially among people who are looking for a spiritual path that is open, accessible and responsive to change.

Deborah Hopkinson
November 1985
Honolulu

Once a monk on pilgrimage met a woman living in a hut. The monk asked, "Do you have any disciples?"

The woman said, "Yes."

The monk said, "Where are they?"

She said, "The mountains, rivers and earth, the plants and trees, are all my disciples."

The monk said, "Are you a nun?"

She said, "What do you see me as?"

He said, "A layperson."

The woman in a hut said, "You can't be a monk!"

The monk said, "You shouldn't mix up Buddhism."

She said, "I'm not mixing up Buddhism."

The monk said, "Aren't you mixing up Buddhism this way?"

She said, "You're a man, I'm a woman—where has there ever been any mixup?"

Women and Buddhist History

The Original Buddhist Women

Susan Murcott

The *Therigatha*, a collection of 73 poems or 522 stanzas, is an anthology of poems by Indian Buddhist nuns who were contemporaries of Buddha.[1] As a record of the words, lives, spiritual achievements, and authority of women at the source of the great religious traditions of the world, it is all but unique. It is a small section in the great canon of Buddhist religious literature. In the language of Pali, theri means "women elders" or "women who have grown old with knowledge; gatha means "verse," "song," or "stanza;" hence the *Therigatha* are poems of the wise women of original Buddhism. These poems are an expression of joy in their achievement of nirvana, the highest goal of their faith. In force and beauty they are fit to rank with the best productions of Indian lyrical poetry, from the hymns of the Rig Veda to the lyrical poems of Kalidasa and Amaru.

While the poems preserve the precious record of the women's actual words, further information about the seventy-two women (a seventy-third poem is attributed to a group of women) can be gleaned from the commentary on the *Therigatha*, the *Paramattha-dipani*. This text furnishes us with the biographical accounts of the nuns. While much in it may be legendary, there is no doubt but that these accounts contain a kernel of historical truth.

The poems and stories together offer the best picture we can gain of the original Buddhist women. The poems and stories which follow are a selection from the *Therigatha* and its commentary. The poems are my translations from the Pali original; the stories are biographical sketches based primarily on the commentary,[2] supplemented with information from other Pali Buddhist sources, and by my own comments.

Mahapajapati Gotami

Mahapajapati Gotami, who was to become the founder of the first order of Buddhist nuns, was born in the Koliyan clan in the town of Devadaha. At her birth, an astrologer foretold that she would be the leader of a large following, and thus she was named Pajapati, meaning "leader of an organized assembly of people." It was further prophesied of her, as it had been of her older sister Maya, that she would be the mother of a secular or religious ruler.

Pajapati and her sister, Maya, were both married to a chief of the Sakyan clan, Suddhodana, and lived with him in the capital town of Kapilavatthu. Frequently, Buddhist legend depicts Suddhodana as a great king, and his son, Siddhartha, as his prince and heir. In fact, in the Sakyan clan, any male was eligible to be chief—it was a position elected by rotation. The only true king of that region was Pasenadi, King of Kosala, who was overlord of the states which included the Sakyan and Koliyan clans. Maya's and Pajapati's marriage was into a clan similar to their own. Both clans were small and did not observe caste distinctions. Clan members worked at agriculture, wielded arms when necessary, and traded in nearby provinces.

Maya was the first to become pregnant. As was customary at the time, Maya wanted to give birth in her family home, so when she was near her time, she undertook the journey to Devadaha. En route, she stopped in the Lumbini Garden to rest and admire the flowering trees. When she raised her arm to pick a branch of an asoka tree, she felt her initial labor pains and gave birth to a boy under the tree. (Over two centuries later, the Buddhist Emperor Asoka set up a pillar to mark that site. Since the pillar survives today, it is possible to identify the place exactly.)

But seven days after her delivery, Maya died. Neither history nor legend tells us why, but Pajapati took Siddhartha and raised him as her own first child, and later bore two more children, a daughter named Sundari-Nanda and a son named Nanda.

Many years passed. At twenty-nine Siddhartha left home and did not return during the six years of his religious quest. His foster mother was in her fifties or early sixties when Siddhartha finally returned to Kapilavatthu. Upon his return, he was treated coolly. The Sakyan clan, known for their pride and religious conservatism, was skeptical of the novel teachings of a once favorite son. Pajapati no doubt would have been sensitive to all the varying reactions. Her own response was to welcome him, and when the Buddha preached to them, both she and her husband were moved by his teachings and became converts.

By this time, Pajapati was not only eminent as the wife of the chieftain, but was also respected for her age. Now as a lay convert to her son's new teachings, she may have been held in even greater esteem as a woman who had direct access to religious instruction and practice.

One by one, or in groups, women sought Pajapati's support, advice, and direction. Her attraction for these women was not merely a matter of status. She shared with them, and after her husband died, she may have exemplified to them, the particular anxiety of being a woman without any primary male relations. Following the Buddha's return to Kapilavatthu, Pajapati's son, Nanda, and her grandnephew Rahula, had both become monks. Not long after this, Suddhodana died. This left Pajapati without the web of family connections that gave every woman in that society her identity and security.

All together, the number of women who had come to Pajapati by this time totaled "five hundred," a phrase frequently used to mean a great many. No doubt some came simply for comfort and support, others came to resolve ultimate questions of birth, suffering, and death, yet others sought a new family with women they trusted and with whom they shared common experience. The longing of these women, whatever form it took, became their spiritual aspiration.

Pajapati recognized the powerful conjunction of events and people. An old but influential woman without further worldly obligations, she was surrounded by displaced wives, widows, dancers, musicians, and courtesans. Lacking other kin, these women were turning to her and to one another. Pajapati decided to take the following course, recounted in the *Cullavagga*:

> Now at one time the Buddha was staying among the Sakyans at Kapilavatthu in the Banyan Monastery. Mahapajapati Gotami went to the place where the Buddha was, approached and greeted him and, standing at a respectful distance, spoke to him:
>
> "It would be good, Lord, if women could be allowed to renounce their homes and enter into the homeless state under the dharma and discipline of the Tathagata."
>
> "Enough, Gotami. Don't set your heart on women being allowed to do so."
>
> (A second and a third time Pajapati made the same request in the same words and received the same reply.) And thinking that the Blessed One would not allow women to enter into homelessness, she bowed to him, and keeping her right side towards him, departed in tears.
>
> Then the Blessed One set out for Vesali. And Pajapati cut off her hair, put on saffron-colored robes, and set out for Vesali with a number of Sakyan women. She arrived at Kutagara Hall in the Great

Grove with swollen feet and covered with dust. Weeping, she stood there outside the Hall.

Seeing her standing there, the venerable Ananda asked, "Why are you crying?"

"Because, Ananda, the Blessed One does not permit women to renounce their homes and enter into the homeless state under the dharma and discipline proclaimed by the Tathagata."

Then the venerable Ananda went to the place where the Buddha was, bowed down before him, and took his seat to one side. And he said to the Blessed One, "Pajapati is standing outside with swollen feet, covered with dust, and crying because you do not permit women to renounce their homes and enter into the homeless state. It would be good, Lord, if women were to have permission to do so."

"Enough, Ananda. Don't set your heart on women being allowed to do so."

(A second and a third time Ananda made the same request in the same words and received the same reply.)

Then Ananda thought: the Blessed One does not give his permission. Let me try asking on other grounds.

"Are women able, Lord, when they have entered into homelessness to realize the fruits of stream-entry, of once-returning, of non-returning, and of arahantship?"

"Yes, Ananda, they are able."

"If women then are able to realize perfection, and since Pajapati was of great service to you—she was your aunt, nurse, foster mother; when your mother died, she even suckled you at her own breast—it would be good if women could be allowed to enter into homelessness."

"If then, Ananda, Pajapati accepts the Eight Special Rules, let that be reckoned as her ordination."[3]

It must have been evident to the Buddha that Pajapati and the group of women with her, who had walked one hundred and fifty miles barefoot, with the shaved heads and saffron-colored robes of the already ordained, would not accept "No" for an answer. The sight of these women and their unshakable sincerity must have made a vivid impression. Their resoluteness was audacious in a culture where humility and obedience were desirable traits in women. Perhaps the Eight Special Rules, the acceptance of which was a prerequisite to women's ordination, were a bulwark against any possible future boldness. Though the Eight Special Rules clearly relegated women to a secondary status, Pajapati accepted them in order to achieve her central goal of establishing an order of nuns.

But later, in a story less frequently told, Pajapati returned with a further request to eliminate the first Special Rule, which required that even the most senior nun bow down to even the youngest novice monk, and thereby undercut the other seven:

> "I would ask one thing of the Blessed One, Ananda. It would be good if the Blessed One would allow making salutations standing up in the presence of another, paying reverence, and the proper performance of duties to take place equally between both bhikkhus and bhikkhunis according to seniority."
>
> And the venerable Ananda went to the Blessed One (and repeated her words to him).
>
> "This is impossible, Ananda, and I cannot allow it. Even those teachers of false dharma don't permit such conduct in relation to women; how much less can the Tathagata allow it?"[4]

In Pajapati's attempt to change the first and most blatently sexist rule, we can understand that she was not in sympathy with the discrimination the rules reflected. Unfortunately, that is all we hear of the politics of the early order of nuns. But we do know a little more about Pajapati. Upon ordination, she received a subject of meditation and through it was able to realize perfection. She writes: "I have reached the state (nirodha) where everything stops," that is, the extinction of sensation, feeling, consciousness. This achievement is synonymous with nirvana, the highest attainment.

At the ripe old age of one hundred and twenty, Pajapati knew that her time of death was near. Though it was against monastic regulations that a sick nun be visited by any monk, Pajapati asked Siddhartha to come to her. He went, thereby changing the rule and giving her the comfort she sought. Miracles occurred at her death and cremation, equalled only by those which took place at Buddha's own death.[5]

We can consider Pajapati and her sister Maya the "Great Mothers" of the Buddhist tradition. For Maya, mother of the Buddha, this is an obvious designation. But it is equally true of Pajapati. Mahapajapati Gotami contains within herself the breadth of experience that makes her the appropriate founding mother of Buddhism.

Mahapajapati Gotami

Homage to you Buddha,
best of all creatures,
who set me and many others
free from pain.

All pain is understood,
the cause, the craving is dried up,
the Noble Eightfold Way unfolds,
I have reached the state where everything stops.

I have been
mother,
son,
father,
brother,
grandmother;
knowing nothing of the truth
I journeyed on.

But I have seen the Blessed One;
this is my last body,
and I will not go
from birth to birth
again.
This is my last rebirth.

Look at the disciples all together,
their energy,
their sincere effort.
This is homage to the buddhas.

Maya gave birth to Gotama
for the sake of us all.
She has driven back the pain
of the sick and the dying.

Dantika

Dantika was from Savatthi, the daughter of the minister of the King of Kosala. She joined the community of nuns under Pajapati. In her poem, the lovely closing line, "I went into the forest and concentrated my mind," connects her with the earliest followers of Gotama, as it was particularly among them that the life of the forest-dwelling renunciant was extolled. In that age, virgin forest covered a great portion of the land surrounding the Ganges River, separating the towns by great distances. Wandering ascetics and yogis who went into the forest for solitude were also supported by the forest; they slept under trees and ate wild foods. "Some followers of the Sakyan (Gotama) dwelt in forests, there to subsist on fruit and roots and to dress in bark and antelope's hides."[6] For this reason, it has been suggested that the emerging Buddhist movement, in common with the whole tradition of wandering renunciants, constituted a return to the old ways of the food-gatherers, the aboriginal forest dwellers.[7]

Dantika went to the forest to carry out her meditation undisturbed. But perhaps she dwelt there as well. References to the solitary life are rare in the poems of the nuns. Some of the early nuns who lived in the forest as hermits were raped, and because of this, it became a rule of the sangha that women could no longer go into the forest alone.[8] But Dantika's poem may predate this rule.

Dantika

As I left my daytime resting place on Vulture Peak,
I saw an elelphant
come up on the riverbank
after its bath.

A man took a hook and said to the elephant,
"Give me your foot."
The elephant stretched out its foot;
the man mounted.

Seeing what was wild before
gone tame under human hands,
I went into the forest
and concentrated my mind.

Bhadda Kundalakesa

Bhadda was born into a financier's family in Rajagaha. One day, as a young woman sitting at her window, she saw a highway robber being led to execution. Falling in love with him at first sight, she begged her father to obtain his release. Out of a misguided love, he did, bribing the guards heavily. Then he had the man bathed, dressed in fine clothes, and brought before her.

The robber's name was Satthuka, and he was the son of a king's minister. Despite his prestigious family background and this opportunity for a new beginning, he remained true to his former trade—he was less interested in Bhadda's love than in the jewels she wore. So he made up this story—that when the city guards were leading him to Robber's Cliff for execution, he had vowed to the cliff deity that if he were spared, he would return and make an offering.

Bhadda prepared such an offering and together they went to the cliff, at his request, leaving her attendants behind. But when they were alone, and he showed neither affection nor gratitude, she began to be afraid.

At the summit of the cliff he said, "Do you really think I have come here to make an offering? What a fool you are! I have come for your jewels." And he told her to remove her outer robe and wrap her jewels inside.

Without hesitation she replied, "Please grant me one wish," and she asked if she could embrace him once before she died. He agreed, and she embraced him first from the front. Then, embracing him from the back, she pushed him over the cliff. For this act, even the deity of the cliff applauded her, praising her keen presence of mind, and saying:

"Wisdom is not always confined to men;
A woman, too, is wise, and shows it now and then."[9]

Afterwards, Bhadda could not face her family. She chose to enter the order of the Svetambara Jains, the first religious sect in history to establish an order of nuns. Asked what level of renunciation she wished to undertake, Bhadda said that she wanted to commit herself to their severest asceticism. Therefore, in one of the austerities of initiation, they tore out her hair.[10]

Eventually, she mastered all the Jain teachings, but she grew dissatisfied and left that sangha, traveling here and there in search of the wisest teachers.

Whenever Bhadda arrived in a new village, she stuck a rose-apple branch in a pile of sand to announce her desire to engage in religious debate. The village children kept watch on that branch to see if anyone would challenge her by knocking it down. If the branch withered while she remained at a village, she would procure a fresh one. After years of this kind of "dharma-encounter," Bhadda could find no equal.

Then one day she came to Savatthi and stuck a rose-apple branch in a pile of sand there. Gotama's leading disciple, Sariputta, lived in Savatthi, and noticing the branch, he asked some children to knock it down. The debate thus established, a crowd of villagers gathered. Bhadda put her questions first, but Sariputta could answer them all with ease, even the most abstruse. Then came his turn and he asked her, "One—what is that?" Bhadda paused, and, not knowing how to respond, asked that he become her teacher. Instead, Sariputta sent her to Gotama, who recognized her depth of understanding and gave her instruction. Hearing his words, she immediately attained enlightenment. Then, in a rare gesture of respect, the Buddha ordained her by simply saying, "Come, Bhadda."

Of this unique ordination, Isabel Horner writes,

> When female novices wished to receive the Upasampada ordination, they had to ask for it from both the Sanghas (the sangha of nuns and of monks). Only one kind of exception to this custom was known, and that was when Gotama himself ordained an entrant by saying, "Come," calling the entrant by name. This kind of ordination is recorded of one woman, Bhadda Kundalakesa, the ex-Jain."[11]

Gotama considered Bhadda first among the nuns in the speed with which she gained the highest truth. But we should not overlook the years of experience that preceded that realization.

In her poem, Bhadda tells of her former austere practices and then of her life as a Buddhist almswoman. Even after her conversion to Buddhism, she seems to have kept her independent, wandering ways.

Bhadda Kundalakesa

I cut my hair and wore the dust,
and I wandered in my one robe,
finding fault where there was none,
and finding no fault where there was.

Then I came from my rest one day
at Vulture Peak
and saw the pure Buddha
with his monks.

I bent my knee,
paid homage,
pressed my palms together.
We were face to face.

"Come Bhadda," he said;
that was my ordination.

I have wandered over Anga and Magadha,
Vajji, Kasi and Kosala;
fifty-five years with no debt,
I have enjoyed the alms of these kingdoms.

A wise lay follower
gained a lot of merit;
he gave a robe to Bhadda
who is free from all bonds.

Patacara

Patacara was born into a banker's family in the town of Savatthi. When she was a young woman, her parents arranged for her to marry a young man of equal rank. But one of the family servants was her lover, and, defying her parents' wishes, she ran away with him and set up house in a remote place.

Months passed and she became pregnant. As her pregnancy came to term, she wanted to go to her parents' home and have their care at the time of birth. Her husband procrastinated, and one day while he was out, she left. He soon discovered what had happened, followed Patacara, and overtook her midway to Savatthi. There, labor set in, she gave birth safely, and together they returned to their dwelling place.

Later, a second child was conceived. Once more, Patacara wanted to return to her parents' home, and once more her husband was reluctant. Again she left without him, taking their child, and again he pursued and caught up with her as her labor was beginning. But this time a great storm rose up. Patacara needed shelter, and her husband, while hurriedly cutting grass and stakes in the forest, was bitten by a poisonous snake and died. Thinking herself abandoned, Patacara gave birth alone, and passed the night lying over her children, using her body to protect them from the storm. In the morning she discovered her husband's body. For a day and night she was paralyzed with grief. When the second day dawned, she again took up the journey to her parents' home.

She came to a river swollen with flood waters. Too weak to carry both children across at once, she took the newborn first. On the far side, she placed the child on a pile of leaves, but was so reluctant to leave him that she looked back again and again. Halfway across the river, she saw a hawk seize her newborn and carry him off. The hawk ignored Patacara's screams, but the older child, thinking his mother was calling him, came up to the river bank, fell in and drowned. Utterly destitute, all Patacara could do was resume her journey.

On the outskirts of Savatthi she met a townsman and asked whether he knew her family. He said, "Don't ask me about them, ask about anything else."

"But there is nothing else I care about," she answered.

And so he said to her, "You saw how the god rained all last night. Last night your family's house collapsed and fell on them, and they are burning on one pyre, the banker, wife and son. You can see the smoke."

With that, Patacara went out of her mind. She wandered around in circles. Her clothing became ragged and fell off. (Her name, which means "cloak-walker," refers to this.) The townspeople drove her off with sticks and refuse.

One day, still mad, still walking around in circles, she entered Jeta Grove where the Buddha was preaching. Those who had gathered to listen wanted to keep her away, but Gotama followed her and put himself in her path. As she encountered him, he said, "Sister, recover your presence of mind." And she recovered her presence of mind.

She saw that she was naked. A man threw her his outer robe. "Help me," she said to the Buddha, and she told him her terrible story.

He replied, "Patacara, don't think you have come to someone who can help you. In your many lives, you have shed more tears for the dead than there is water in the four oceans." This made her grief somehow less heavy. He went on to say that when she herself went to another world, no kin could help, that even in this world, no kin can help. And he spoke of the Buddhist path. When he had finished, she asked if she could be ordained. Together they went to the community of nuns, and she was accepted there.

Patacara's poem recounts an experience that takes place later. It speaks of the moment of her enlightenment experience. Almost no other poem within the *Therigatha* is so precise in describing such a moment. We see a sequence of events familiar in the Buddhist contemplative tradition—a period of intense concentration, relaxation after that concentration, and a catalyst from outside—the going out of the lamp—that sparks her breakthrough.

Patacara

When they plough their fields
and sow seeds in the earth,
when they care for their wives and children,
young brahmans find riches.

But I've done everything right
and followed the rule of my teacher.
I'm not lazy or proud.
Why haven't I found peace?

Bathing my feet
I watched the bath water
spill down the slope.
I concentrated my mind
the way you train a good horse.

Then I took a lamp
and went into my cell,
checked the bed,
and sat down on it.
I took a needle
and pushed the wick down.

When the lamp went out
my mind was freed.

Notes to the Text

[1]Richard Pischel, ed. *The Therigatha* (London: published for the Pali Text Society by Luzae and Co. Ltd., 1966).

[2]Caroline Rhys Davids, *Psalms of the Sisters* (London: published for the Pali Text Society by Henry Fronde, Oxford University Press Warehouse, 1909).

[3]This long passage is my adaptation of the *Cullavagga* X, 1, 1-4, from two English translations: Max Muller, ed., *Vinaya Texts*. Translated by T. W. Rhys Davids and Hermann Oldenberg. *Sacred Books of the East*. Vol. XX, Part III (Oxford: Clarendon Press, 1885), pp. 320-322; and I. B. Horner, trans., *The Book Discipline*. Vol. V (London: Luzac and Co., 1952) pp. 352-354.

[4]This is my adaptation of the *Cullavagga* X, 3.1. from Max Muller, ed., *Vinaya Texts*. Translated by T. W. Rhys Davids and Hermann Oldenberg. *Sacred Books of the East*. Vol. XX, Part III (Oxford: Clarendon Press, 1885) pp. 327-328.

[5]According to the Buddhist faith, the Buddha did not die. The appropriate concept to express his changed condition is the term *parinibbana*. It means "full nibbana" and is the extinction of the elements of mind and body, the *khandhas*.

[6]I.B. Horner, trans. *The Book of Discipline* (*Suttavibhanga*) Vol. I-III (London: Oxford

University Press Warehouse, 1938, 1940, 1942) p. xxix.

[7]D. D. Kosambi, *Ancient India* (New York: World Publishing Co., 1969) p. 104.

[8]Max Muller, ed. *Vinaya Texts*. Translated by T. W. Rhys Davids and Hermann Oldenberg. *Sacred Books of the East,* Vol. XX (Oxford: Clarendon Press, 1885) p. 362. (Vinaya x, 23.)

[9]E. W. Burlingame, *Buddhist Legends: The Dhammadapa Commentary,* Harvard Oriental Series, Vol. 28. (Cambridge: Harvard University Press, 1921) p. 229.

[10]This is the practice of loya, "up-rooting the hair from the head." See S. C. Deo, *History of Jaina Monaahism*, (Poona: Deccan College, 1956).

[11]I. B. Horner, *Women Under Primitive Buddhism* (London: George Poutledge and Sons, Ltd., 1930), pp. 213-214.

Kanzeon
Robert Aitken

Cho nen Kanzeon;
bo nen Kanzeon.

Mornings my thought is Kanzeon;
evenings my thought is Kanzeon.

—*Enmei Jikku Kannon Kyo*

Kanzeon, or Kannon, is Kuan-yin in Chinese, a derivation of Avalokiteshvara, the Indian Bodhisattva. Avalokiteshvara's name means "the Lord who looks down," implying the Lord who looks over all being compassionately.[1] This meaning changed with the transition of the archetype into China, and Kuan-yin, or Kanzeon became "the one who hearkens to the sounds of the world." In this change from looking downward to listening closely, the Bodhisattva also evolved from a male to a female, or at least androgenous, figure.

One gets the sense that in looking down, Avalokiteshvara observes, while in listening closely, Kanzeon feels. In Buddhist art one finds the male Avalokiteshvara in meditative poses, sometimes holding symbols of wisdom, while the female Kanzeon commonly holds a jar of healing water and willow branch for dispensing it to all beings.

Archetypes tend to change when they cross cultural lines. The Christ of Cuidad Juarez is not the Christ of El Paso. The male Avalokiteshvara became the female Kanzeon (and the female Tibetan equivalent Tara) with the Chinese and Tibetan view of compassion as a female attribute. Starting afresh with the archetype, it probably seemed natural to them to portray her as a woman.[2]

Kanzeon meets religious needs of Far Eastern peoples, and is the central figure in many Buddhist temples, including those of Zen. The long *Kannon Sutra* (Chapter 25 of the Lotus Sutra) is recited daily in devout households and temples all over Japan. I once attended a funeral service that was led by priests of Zen, Nichiren, and Shingon sects, representing the three affiliations of family members. They recited the long *Kannon Sutra* in unison without opening their sutra books, clearly in harmony with one another.

At Ryutakuji (where I trained long ago) I particularly enjoyed the recitation of the long *Kannon Sutra* on sacred days that fall at the beginning and middle of each month, an inheritance from the lunar calendar, when the new moon appeared on the first day of the month and the full moon on the fifteenth. On those days there are sutras in the main hall in the early morning as usual, but then the monks and others in residence troop around to the various shrines on the compound, and recite sutras at each of them, including one at the very top of the hill behind the temple. We would climb up the hill on the stepping stones in our clogs, and crowding into a tiny room would recite the *Kannon Sutra* to the syncopated beat of a big drum. What a marvelous din it was!

Here is a portion of the sutra in D.T. Suzuki's translation—the interlocutor is Aksayamati Bodhisattva, pronounced Mujini Bosatsu in Japanese (I have changed Dr. Suzuki's gender forms to the female):

> Mujini Bosatsu said to the Buddha, "World Honored One, how does Kanzeon Bosatsu visit this Saha world?" (The Sahaloka is the world of patience, the world of suffering.) "How does she practice the Dharma for all beings? What is the extent of her skillful means?"
>
> The Buddha said to Mujini Bosatsu, "Oh good man, if there are beings in any country who are to be saved by her assuming a Buddha-form, Kanzeon Bosatsu will manifest herself in the form of a Buddha and preach them the Dharma. If beings are to be saved by her assuming a Pratyekya-Buddha-form, the Bosatsu will manifest herself in the form of a Pratyekya-Buddha and preach them the Dharma. If beings are to be saved by her assuming a Sravaka-form, the Bosatsu will manifest herself in the form of a Sravaka and preach them the Dharma....If beings are to be saved by her assuming an Isvara-form, the Bosatsu will manifest herself in the form of an Isvara and preach them the Dharma. If beings are to be saved by her assuming a Mahesvara-form, the Bosatsu will manifest herself in the form of a Mahesvara and preach them the Dharma.... If beings are to be saved by her assuming a householder's form, the Bosatsu will manifest herself in the form of a householder and preach them the Dharma. If beings are to be saved by her assum-

> ing a lay disciple's form, the Bosatsu will manifest herself in the form of a lay disciple and preach them the Dharma. If beings are to be saved by her assuming a state-officer's form, the Bosatsu will manifest herself in the form of a state-officer and preach them the Dharma. If beings are to be saved by her assuming a Brahman form, the Bosatsu will manifest herself in the form of a Brahman and preach them the Dharma....If beings are to be saved by her assuming a female form of the family of a householder, or a lay-disciple, or a state-officer, or a Brahman, the Bosatsu will manifest herself in the form of such a female and preach them the Dharma....If beings are to be saved by her assuming a Deva-, Naga-, Yaksa-, Gandharva-, Asursa-, Garuda-, Kinnara-, Mahoraga-, Manusya-, or Amanusya-form, the Bosatsu will manifest herself in any of these forms and preach them the Dharma."[3]

The marvelous rhythm that comes with this recitation in the Sino-Japanese with its monosyllabic form, together with the big mokugyo or the drum, makes it a truly moving sutra, and I can understand that for some people the recitation of this sutra alone would be enough for their devotional practice.

When I was a young Zen student living in Kamakura, I often visited the Hasei Kannon Temple near the Daibutsu. The Daibutsu (Great Buddha) is a popular tourist attraction, but the Hasei Kannon Temple is not so well known. It is a bit off the main street, and in those days, 35 years ago, it was visited almost entirely by devotees. An enormous image of Kanzeon, carved from a single cedar log, dominated the large hall. One day I felt a little embarrassed by my presence at the devotions of one of the pilgrims, an elderly layman. He stood before Kanzeon, reciting by heart her long sutra, which takes twenty minutes. I felt as though I were intruding on his deep devotion and his deep belief—the oneness with Kanzeon he expressed so vividly with his body and low voice.

In Chinese and Japanese devotional painting and sculpture, Kanzeon is a noble figure, sometimes with a child in her arms, sometimes surrounded by children, or with youthful attendants. She appears in the Sahaloka, the world of patience and suffering, and guides us to an understanding of suffering, from endurance to consent to delight in this temporary existence. She shows us that patience is far more than just making a virtue of necessity.

Kanzeon is the Bodhisattva of Compassion because she is in tune with sounds of the world. These sounds confirm Kanzeon. Dogen Zenji said, "The ten thousand things advance and confirm the self, and that is enlightenment."[4] Kanzeon is confirmed, realized, enlightened by those sounds: a dog barking, an airplane flying overhead, even the neighbor's radio; and not only sounds—also smells, things that are seen, tasted, felt, and so on. Occasions for reception are continually coming.

We venerate and supplicate Kanzeon, but she is also our practice. This is the second transformation of Avalokiteshvara in the Mahayana. In the epigraph, I quote my translation of key lines from the *Enmei Jikku Kannon Kyo*: "Mornings my thought is Kanzeon; evenings my thought is Kanzeon," meaning, my way of zazen and daily life is Kanzeon, thought after thought, moment by moment.

The lines can still be understood devotionally. D.T. Suzuki translates them: "Every morning our thoughts are on Kanzeon; every evening our thoughts are on Kanzeon,"[5] which places her "out there." But if we are to complete the personalization process begun in the Chinese Mahayana, then I think the lines can be understood more intimately: "Mornings I hear the sounds of the world; evenings I hear the sounds of the world." The dove, the mynah, and the thrush advance and confirm me. The sound of the wind, the faraway sounds of traffic, advance and confirm me—just as the sound of a stone striking a bamboo stalk confirmed Hsiang-yen—just as the sight of the Morning Star confirmed the Buddha. When you are hearing the sounds of the world, you are not thinking anything. There is only that dimension of sounds and you yourself disappear. You are confirmed by those sounds because your body and mind have fallen away.[6]

Kanzeon is a Bodhisattva, an enlightened being, who becomes the sound of others passing through the world, who becomes one with each animal and plant and person, and thus suffers with them. Bassui Zenji asked, "Who is hearing that sound?"[7] When you work on Mu or on breath counting, and are completely one with your practice, then at that depth the song of the thrush comes right through, the squeak of the window comes right through, and in special times you find the sound originates in your own body. To do zazen is to be vulnerable and to find that the outside is not outside.

However, if you are thinking something there on your cushion, then you have forgotten Mu. You have forgotten your breath counting. Your thoughts are defenses shutting out the world. Sometimes people use Mu as defense, and when thoughts come, they say firmly, "Mu, Mu." They push them away with Mu. That might be necessary at times, I suppose, as a temporary device. But it is not the most fruitful way to practice Mu. Sitting there as Kanzeon, let Mu be your thought, and the other stuff will die down.

I am not condemning thought. Thought is mind itself. It is important, however, to understand how thought by itself is limited. When you think something, then you are projecting yourself. You are excluding the thing, and limiting yourself to yourself. You are not letting the thing be your thought. But when you suffer the thing to come, then you are letting the thing be your thought. Then Mu is your thought—then the birdsong and Mu are not two things. This is an important point. I will stop you in dokusan when you are talking *about* something. I want to experience the thing.

Anne and I were once very close to a young woman who was in and out of the Hawaii State Hospital. She would live with us for a while, and then she would have to go back to the hospital. When she was released again, she would come and live with us once more. This went on for several years and she was like a daughter to us. One day when I was walking beside the road on my way to the university, I saw her coming toward me. She was looking down at the path, walking straight ahead, and she didn't see me at all. When we were abreast, I said, "Hello," and she was startled and cried out. She was so absorbed in her thoughts that she was completely encapsulated.

I think there's only a relative difference between such an extreme state of self-absorption and the thinking, remembering, fantasizing, scheming, storytelling, and so on, that we indulge in when we are on our cushions. We are all a little crazy, at least.

Sakyamuni Buddha may have had a wandering thought once in a while. On the other hand, we are all of us realized, and we have all had moments when we listened to the other and forgot ourselves. Our thoughts were quiet, and there was just the other conveying an impression. The archetype of this condition is Kanzeon. How old is Kanzeon? This is a good checking question for you.

When you confine Kanzeon to the altar or to books of Buddhist art, then you are missing the chance to mature as Kanzeon herself or himself—and to cultivate the power of her compassion. Just as the image of Kanzeon evolved through Buddhist history in various stages so you as Kanzeon can mature with earnest practice through your lifetime and beyond.

This is not just a matter of zazen, dokusan, and teisho. Do you really listen to others? Do you listen to your children, to your spouse, to your friends? Look at the textbooks on parenting and family therapy that are appearing these days. They all stress the importance of listening while forgetting the self.

But is our practice confined to listening? Not at all. Here again we can learn from the way Kanzeon is presented. The thousand-armed Kanzeon holds a thousand implements of work. That is to say, a thousand implements of upaya, a thousand implements of compassion. A pen, a hoe, a pan, and so on, all of them skillful means for saving others. Kanzeon is you and I coming forth to engage in the process of enlightening bushes and grasses and all the many beings of the world.

Classical Buddhism sets forth the truth of mutual interdependence. Kanzeon is the Mahayana archetype of mutual support, giving life and fulfillment to the Sangha process, the Sangha of stones and clouds, the Sangha of wild creatures and forests, the Sangha of people in Africa and Southeast Asia and the slums and prisons of our cities, not to mention our own families and friends.

Enmei Jikku Kannon Kyo

Kanzeon	Oh, Kanzeon!
namu Butsu	veneration to the Buddha!
yo Butsu u in	with Buddha I have origin;
yo Butsu u en	with Buddha I have affinity;
Buppo so en	affinity with Buddha, Dharma, and Sangha;
jo raku ga jo	eternity, joy, self, and purity.
cho nen Kanzeon	mornings my thought is Kanzeon;
bo nen Kanzeon	evenings my thought is Kanzeon;
nen nen ju shin ki	thought after thought arises in mind;
nen nen fu ri shin	thought after thought is not separate from mind.

[1]Edward Conze, *Buddhism: Its Essence and Development* (New York: Harper and Brothers, 1959), p. 147.
[2]John Blofeld, *Bodhisattva of Compassion: The Mystical Tradition of Kuan Yin* (Boulder: Shambala, 1978), p. 41.
[3]D.T. Suzuki, *Manual of Zen Buddhism* (New York: Grove Press, 1960), pp. 32-34.
[4]Hakuyu Taizan Maezumi, *The Way of Everyday Life* (Los Angeles: Center Publications, 1978), n.p.
[5]Suzuki, *Manual of Zen Buddhism*, p. 15.
[6]John Blofeld does not discuss personalization of Kanzeon in his otherwise interesting study, *Boddhisattva of Compassion*.
[7]"Bassui's Sermon on One-Mind and Letters to His Disciples," *The Three Pillars of Zen*, ed. Philip Kapleau (Boston: Beacon Press, 1967), p. 172.

The Kahawai Koans

Deborah Hopkinson and Susan Murcott

In 1980, noted Chinese translator Thomas Cleary shared with Robert Aitken and the *Kahawai* collective material he had collected from original Chinese and Japanese sources in which women were leading characters. Since women rarely appear in the typical roles of earnest disciples or enlightened teachers in classical koans, these new discoveries were a great delight. These koans, informally dubbed the "*Kahawai* Koans," were published in several issues of the journal beginning in 1981. In addition, several students in the Diamond Sangha practicing with Aitken Roshi took up these stories as part of their formal Zen training.

Koans are perhaps the most misunderstood aspect of Zen Buddhism. Many people have heard the phrase "the sound of one hand clapping," but most people have only a vague idea of a koan as some conundrum, or paradox, which is somehow resolved in a gesture or response as enigmatic as the original question. Even students of Zen themselves are often confused about the role of koan study within a particular school of Zen, and look upon it as something obscure or unattainable.

Koan study, like other experiential things—learning how to swim, for example—is difficult to explain in words. It's a lot easier to get in the water and just swim. By seeing koan study in its historical and religious context, we can gain a better appreciation of the meaning and purpose of the koan in Zen training. This, in turn, provides a basis for understanding the role of women in the koan tradition and the corresponding importance of the *Kahawai* Koans.

Shakyamuni Buddha experienced realization through a long search which focused on a personal question: "Why is there suffering?" This question served as a natural theme of his meditation and a focus for his existential questioning, and in this sense we may call it a koan. When Buddhism spread from India to China 500 or more years after the Buddha's death, Chinese teachers probably also used their own personal expressions of this universal searching, and drew from the body of available Indian Buddhist literature, as well as from their own indigenous Taoist philosophy to provide meditation themes.

As the new religious practice gradually took hold and grew, Chinese teachers began to pose questions for their students, and to use sayings, anecdotes and scriptural quotes of the past to provide a focus for meditation and to test a student's insight. Usually one teacher had so many students that these dialogues took place in public in the Dharma hall. The word koan itself is made up of two Chinese characters—*ko*, meaning public, and *an*, meaning records or cases.

These "public cases"—dialogues, questions, and anecdotes, began to be cultivated and handed down by about the turn of the 9th century during the T'ang period. Although broad generalizations about the specific use and development of the koan are not possible because of the enormous variations that existed from teacher to teacher, we do know that collections of koans were already being made by the middle of the 10th century, some of them including poems and comments added by the compiler. This period from the late eighth to the mid-tenth century, a time of great vitality and growth coinciding with the early T'ang period, has been called the Golden Age of Zen.

From about the 10th century through the 13th or 14th century, spontaneous dialogues and encounters appear to have become less frequent and vital, and the use of koans as formalized teaching devices increased. A rich literature developed, much of it drawn from actual or remembered events in the lives of teachers who lived during the previous era. The koan literature intact today derives primarily from collections compiled during this period, which include the *Mumonkan,* the *Hekiganroku* and the *Shoyoroku*, among others.

Today, in schools of Zen which use koan study (and not all do), beginning students are given an initial koan to work with, which, like Shakyamuni's questions, serves as a natural focus for meditation and for the student's existential and religious quest. One of the most commonly used beginning koans is the koan "Mu." (Mu is a Japanese word implying negative, like "un.")

A monk asked Joshu, "Has a dog Buddha nature or not?"

Joshu replied, "Mu."

The student takes up the word "Mu" in zazen, keying the breath to "Mu" becoming completely absorbed in "Mu." Rather than public dialogues, the regular practice includes private interviews between student and teacher, called in Japanese, dokusan, which implies "to work alone with the teacher." Resolution of this first koan, which may take years, is called kensho, the experience of seeing into one's own nature. This experience has been described as "body and mind fall away." In this dimension there is no time and space, I and you, past and future, woman and man.

With this first experience of realization, teacher and student continue to use koans as a means to clarify insights and deepen the practice. While practices differ from teacher to teacher, many continue to rely upon the compilations of koans which are part of the written Zen tradition. Situations and problems from everyday life may also be used. Some schools of Zen may also use koans as a kind of "scripture," from which Buddhist philosophy may be discussed. However, sitting with the koan as a meditation theme, and presenting the resolution in the dokusan room, continue to be the fundamental use of koan practice.

Koans contain stories about the great luminaries in Zen history, and function in many ways as the folklore of the tradition. However, it is overwhelmingly a folklore of men. Very little is known about the women who practiced Zen during its Golden Age. Of the hundreds of koans in the compilations, we can identify only a few women by name, such as Ryutetsuma and Myoshin, and even the anonymous women that appear are few in number.

This lack of role models and female figures can be explained historically, of course, by understanding the position of women in China and Japan during the periods when koans were first written down. Today, however, women come to Zen practice with the expectation of equal access to the full range of practice and leadership opportunities as men. And both women and men need and are entitled to women role models in Zen. We need women we can recognize as guides and leaders—women whose attributes, names and personalities we know—women who can teach us.

The *Kahawai* Koans translated by Thomas Cleary bring to light previously unknown women who were contemporaries of some of the most renowned Zen masters. In many of these koan stories, the women remain anonymous; the stories appear to have been written down as events in the life of the male Zen personage. Other women are named, but unfortunately little else is known about them. But the fact that we have this record at all provides clear evidence of the existence of enlightened, strong, women active and respected in the tradition during the T'ang and Sung periods. While these women remain shadowy folk figures, this record is nevertheless an important contribution to both the Zen tradition and to the literature of feminist spirituality.

Zen history is indeed a folklore, and many of the stories that make up its literature are closer to myth than actual fact. If models of women cannot be found in the tradition, perhaps we need to improvise from the material at hand in order to provide contemporary Zen Buddhists with a non-sexist tradition that is rich and balanced. More research may still uncover the history that is there. And at the same time, contemporary women, by their full participation in Zen, are creating their own stories of women in Zen. To that we can add these stories of women from the past.

The stories presented below are from the *Kahawai* Koans, which include approximately two dozen koans. Some of them are in the traditional dialogue form, while others are narrative accounts of a woman's life.

The Woman Who Lived in a Hut

Once a monk on pilgrimage met a woman living in a hut. The monk asked, "Do you have any disciples?"

The woman said, "Yes."

The monk said, "Where are they?"

She said, "The mountains, rivers and earth, the plants and trees, are all my disciples."

The monk said, "Are you a nun?"

She said, "What do you see me as?"

He said, "A layperson."

The woman in a hut said, "You can't be a monk!"

The monk said, "You shouldn't mix up Buddhism."

She said, "I'm not mixing up Buddhism."

The monk said, "Aren't you mixing up Buddhism this way?"

She said, "You're a man, I'm a woman—where has there ever been any mixup?"

The Tiger

Once when Joshu (Zhaozhou) went out, he saw a woman hoeing a field; he said to her, "What would you do if you suddenly met a fierce tiger?"

She said,. "Nothing can impinge upon my feelings."

Joshu made a spitting sound; she also made a spitting sound.

Joshu said, "There's still this."

Joshu was one of the greatest of Zen masters. Robert Aitken, Zen teacher of the Diamond Sangha in Honolulu, commented that of all the stories in which Joshu appears, and there are many, this is the closest that Joshu ever came to saying, "Yes, good." We can imagine he may have taken many walks near his neighbor's farm to enjoy the company of this equal. This dialogue is an example of the freedom and playfullness that characterizes many Zen koans. How can you show your intimacy with a tiger? With your boss? With a hungry child?

Bamboo Shoots

Joshu asked a woman, "Where are you going?"
She said, "I'm going to filch some of Joshu's bamboo shoots."
Joshu said, "What if you should meet up with Joshu?"
She gave him a slap and he desisted.

Lodging

One evening a woman came into Joshu's temple. Joshu said, "What are you doing?"
She said, "Lodging."
Joshu said, "What place is this?"
She laughed aloud and left.

Perhaps these women are the same as the woman from the field, or perhaps there were many accomplished laywomen in Joshu's sangha. We can imagine women eager to practice with a master of Joshu's reputation, fitting their practice in between long hours of farm and household chores, childrearing and cooking.

These dialogues may seem strange at first. Over the centuries Zen has developed a specialized language, a kind of shorthand to deal with an experience that truly cannot be put into words. With that experience, Joshu's seemingly simple and ordinary questions, "What are you doing?" "Where are you going?" become challenges for these women, and for us, to be answered from the grounds of our deepest selves. Even without that experience, it is easy to see that our ancient mothers could handle themselves with ease in their confrontations with the famous old monk.

Asan

Asan was from Shinano, Japan. She associated with the Soto Zen master Tetsumon and was greatly enlightened. Later she called on Hakuin.

Asan concentrated deeply on Zen. One day during her morning sitting she heard the crow of the rooster and her mind suddenly opened. She said, "The fields, the mountains, the flowers and my body too are the voice of the bird—what is left that can be said to hear?"

When Hakuin was invited to Shinano, Asan went to see him. Hakuin confronted her with "the sound of one hand." Asan immediately said, "Even better than hearing Hakuin's sound of one hand, clap both hands and do your business." Hakuin also drew a picture of a bamboo broom and gave it to Asan. Asan wrote on it, "Sweeping away all the bad teachers in Japan—first of all, Hakuin." Hakuin smiled.

When Asan's sickness in her old age became serious, her sons and daughters surrounded her seeking some last words. Asan laughed and said, "In this world, where not even a drop of dew on a leaf of grass remains, what word or saying should I leave?" Then she serenely passed away.

Several stories in the Cleary tradition give up glimpses into women who studied with the renowned Japanese Zen master Hakuin. Clearly, Asan had a reputation in her time, for this story reveals key points in her Zen career, including her realization experience, dialogue with her teacher, and her parting words.

Women in the World of Zen

Michele Martin

Every religion provides role models in the form of gods, saints, Bodhisattvas, great teachers, heroines, or heroes. The variety is large enough to encompass a range of personalities that reflect basic human characteristics so that each person can find a figure that feels close, familiar, intimate to his or her being. These images function in an intermediate realm between the "human" and "divine" and reflect our deepest desires to become one with the perfect being that in our clearest, most intense moments we know exists.

From one point of view, these figures are not ultimate, but guides along the path. Up the mountain we move towards them, and down the mountain we move through them to manifest in the world. At the place of the absolute, however, there are no roles, no one to play a role, for they have all been transcended in seeing their essence as empty. The one who goes up the mountain, therefore, is not the same as the one who comes down. Further, the particular role we manifest will change as our being freely encounters different situations. In this sense, the figures are mere outlines or suggestions. We make them real in our own way.

These images, then, occupy an intermediate place between what we are as particular individuals and the absolute. In terms of the theory of the threefold body of the Buddha, the role models derive from the Nirmanakaya (actual historical figures) and the Samboghakaya (bliss or reward body) levels. These forms are helpful on stages of our path, but we must never become so attached to them that we stop there and go no further. The references in Zen texts to killing the Buddha point to this problem. With this caveat in mind, we can look again at role models as the configuration of diverse aspects of our own being; these figures should never be taken as something outside ourselves, as transcendent or beyond the immediate experience of our being. If we understand this, then it can be helpful to look at female religious figures as guides, as gateways into our deeper selves.

In every major world religion there are female figures who play an important part in their respective traditions. It is quite revealing, then, to turn to Zen Buddhism and look for anything similar. In the best known texts, such as the *Mumonkan* or *Hekiganroku*, what do we find? Old ladies. Difficult old ladies who ask the right question at the wrong time for the monk concerned. Laudably accurate and clear in their old age, they are hardly apt role models for the lifetime of a woman, unless she is bent on a lonely eccentricity. Further, we know very little about these women, just one small incident in their long lives. They function, therefore, as catalysts in a man's self-realization. They wield the sword of the absolute. Timely arrivals on a male's path, these old women disappear as soon as they have done their (usually devastating) deed. We are given nothing of their personal history or experience, nothing that would encourage us to identify with them for more than this short event. The old ladies appear for a moment, deliver their lines, and vanish.

Two incidents from the Rinzai and Soto traditions reveal something of the Zen attitude toward women. The first case is the familiar story of Tokusan. Burdened with his commentaries on the *Diamond Sutra*, Tokusan was traveling around China to eradicate the heretical teaching of a "special transmission from mind to mind independent of words and outside the scriptures."[1]

> One day he stopped and talked to an old woman who sold tenjin (a kind of cake, the Chinese characters for which can also mean "to light up the mind"). The old woman said, "Venerable Monk, what books do you carry in your box?"
>
> Tokusan said, "They are notes and commentaries on the *Diamond Sutra*."
>
> The old woman said, "It is said in the sutra that the past mind is unattainable, the present mind is unattainable, the future mind is unattainable. Which mind, Venerable Monk, are you going to light up?"
>
> Tokusan was unable to answer this question and had to shut his mouth tight. Even so, he could not die the Great Death at the old woman's words and finally asked, "Is there a Zen teacher in the neighborhood?"
>
> The old woman replied, "Master Ryutan lives five miles away." Arriving at Ryutan's monastery, he was completely defeated.[2]

The old woman put Tokusan to the test and he failed despite long years of study. How did he fail? What was the old woman asking? She asked, "Show me the mind that is beyond time! Manifest your true self." Tokusan could not lose his time-bound self; he could not die the Great Death and stood dumbfounded. This pause shows Tokusan's perplexity and realization of his own inadequacy. To our delight, old women often function in this way, pointing unceremoniously at the holes. Tokusan then asks, "Is there a Zen teacher in the neighborhood?" It is as if he just realized he was sick and called out, "Is there a doctor in the house?"

The incident with the old woman opened Tokusan's way to enlightenment, which occurred when Ryutan, the local Zen teacher, blew out a candle. But what about the old woman? She is still at the roadside stand, and we hear nothing more about her. Nor do we know how she came to her own realization that permitted her to ask such (im)pertinent questions. Her personal history and individual experience are left blank and there is nothing that would allow us to identify with her in the broader sense of a role model. It is the single aspect of her directness and accuracy that we appreciate. Did she study with the local roshi? What was it in her own life that allowed her to come to such an understanding? What practice did she go through? Many questions to be answered, yet all that lingers is a certain affection for this spunky character.

> When the Master (Tozan) first set out on pilgrimage, he met an old woman carrying water. The master asked for some water to drink. The old woman replied, "I will not stop you from drinking, but I have a question which I must ask you first. Tell me, how dirty is water?"
>
> "Water is not dirty at all," said the Master.
>
> "Go away and don't contaminate my water buckets," she answered.[3]

In his commentary, Seizan Yanagida writes that "dirty" refers to women and the five states they cannot attain because they inhabit a female form: Brahma, Sakra, Yama, Dharmachakra, and Buddha. Basically this means that in the Buddhist world, women are upwardly (or inwardly) mobile only to a certain extent. The upper echelons of consciousness are closed, and to enter, women must await rebirth in a proper male form. In this traditional sense, women are limited and thereby discouraged from the very outset of their practice. For contemporary women, this is hard, if not impossible, to accept.

A closer analysis of this dialogue between Tozan and the old woman will illustrate how Zen, though radically non-dualistic, is bound by the very fundamental dualism of male and female. What question is the old woman really asking? Is she fishing for the venerable monk's approval? A kindly pat on her shoulder to tell her she is really all right? Hardly. Here, true to her function, the old woman has found another lacuna, this time filled with a banal morality that posits good and evil, pure and impure. In asking, "How dirty is the water?" she has offered Tozan the opportunity to manifest true self by going beyond the (dirty) half of the dualism she has stated. The mode of the question is the same as the Sixth Patriarch's question to Myo: "Think neither good nor evil. At such a moment, what is the true self of the monk Myo?"[4] In the same vein, the Heart Sutra says: "All things are characterized with emptiness: they are not born, they are not annihilated; they are not tainted, they are not immaculate."

Tozan failed in that he allowed himself to be caught by a dualistic mind, by discriminating consciousness. Therefore, however liberal and open-minded his answer may at first appear, it is in fact slander, for he still sees the old woman as impure and compensates by saying she is pure. In affirming one half of the duality, he maintains the other. The old woman sees this immediately and tells him not to contaminate her buckets. Contaminate with what? The impurity of his own mind that still sees her as an object, half of a duality. So the real situation is actually the reverse of what it might appear: not the lady, but Tozan himself is unclean, polluted by his own inability to transcend the male/female dichotomy and its connotations (in his own mind) of pure and impure.

The critique of Tozan can apply to the history of Zen as well: they have both failed to accept women on an equal footing in this world. From the two cases above, a pattern emerges. Women are incidental and problematic; further, in its treatment of women Zen has, with few exceptions, chosen to see women as outsiders. Throughout its history, Zen has made an object of women, has fallen into the same unenlightened dualism that its very tenets would deny.

In Zen theory, at least, there is an equality of men and women. It is the place of no duality, of absolute true self. And yet there is also the place of a particular self, based on true self. This particular self has to manifest as a form, as a participant in duality and separation. This participation means to be fully human, which is perhaps the most difficult thing to do. This very world, which cannot be denied, is the place of man and woman, of human relationships. How is it then, that Zen has practically ignored the feminine half of the world? How can a religion, or any view of the world, claim to have relevance to all humanity, vow to save all sentient beings, to become absolutely one with everything, to see all as Buddha, and pass by women? It won't do to say that women must simply wait to be reborn as men. This avoids, by shunting off into the future, the whole question of women who are practicing right now, the experience of their individual lives, and their very real desire for enlightenment.

The whole situation would seem rather dismal if Zen is seen as an unchanging set of beliefs and concerns. Yet, as we know, the Buddhisms of India, China, Tibet, and Japan differ. Within Japanese history itself, Zen has undergone many permutations. So we can see this lack of feminine role models and history from another point of view: the absence is an opportunity, a challenge to create from our own experience the understanding of what it means to be a woman and practice Zen. The questions that women (and men) face are vital and essential to every living being as well as crucial for the future of Zen itself. In all of our changing social roles, how do we relate to others in an open, non-manipulative way that affirms freedom and unity, separation and oneness? Do women's minds really function differently? Is our body affected by the practice in a different way than a man's? Is a woman's way to enlightenment the same as a man's? How do we raise our children and give them the opportunity to know themselves truly? Who are our female role models? Perhaps these questions and others can elicit a new form, a new way of understanding through Zen that will better fit our contemporary world.[5]

If we as women can make the first revolution of ourselves into no-self, then will come the second revolution, in which the practice of Zen will evolve to include women as equals in all ways. This process, however, must be based on personal experience, practice, and a deep understanding of ourselves as truly free and truly involved in both the world of no-self and the world of self, which are, indeed, the same, the one complete world.

Author's Postscript

This article was written about ten years ago when I was studying and practicing Zen in Kyoto. The writing was an attempt to come to terms with a pervasive discrimination against women, that I encountered both in this country and in Japan. Involved in the founding of a Zen center, I had gone to Japan hoping to gain an understanding of how Buddhism was transmitted from country to country. If I could know better the cultural patterns of Japan, perhaps it would be easier to discern how Zen practice could be adapted to the West.

For a year, I lived in a Zen temple practicing meditation and immersing myself in the language and culture. Afterwards I moved to an apartment, continuing to practice, attending sesshin, studying tea ceremony, and working with Professors Gadjin Nagao and Keiji Nishitani. These teachers were a great inspiration and opened many new paths.

After two years, I returned to the United States to continue practice, but found that the changes I had undergone in Japan made it difficult to remain within the framework of traditional Zen. At that time, I happened to meet with teachers of Tibetan Buddhism. In this context, I was able to find a focus that fulfilled my personal needs: an emphasis on compassion and faith, the confirmation of the intellect as a tool for practice, and an affirmation of the feminine on a metaphysical, psychological, and concrete level through many female forms: Prajnaparamita, Tara, Vajra Yogini, Yeshe Tsogyal, and others. In union with the masculine, they are the embodiment of wisdom, inseparable from all-embracing compassion.

On an ultimate level, the teachings of Zen and Tibetan Buddhism are the same—the clear empty mind that is not different from form; form that is not different from emptiness. In this sense, the years of Zen practice continue uninterrupted, and my wish to bring all resources to the path and to unfold the feminine has found a home.

Woodstock, New York
June, 1985

Footnotes:

[1]Katsuki Sekida, *Two Zen Classics,* New York, 1977, p. 28.

[2]Zenkei Shibayama, *Zen Comments on the Mumokan*, New York, 1974, p. 209.

[3]*Tozanroku, 26*, published in *Sekai No Meicho, Zengoroku*, vol. 3, with commentary by Seizan Yanagida, and translated by William Powell.

[4]Shibayama, op. cit., p. 172.

[5]Perhaps we will have to go outside the tradition of Zen Buddhism, but not outside our own experience or practice, to find answers. In terms of role models, for example, other religious traditions are rich in female figures. Erich Neumann's *The Mothers* is a classic study of feminine religious archetypes from all over the world. His typology proposes four major categories that reflect the cycle of the seasons. With his outline as a guide, we can draw the following circle: Quan Yin (the female form of Avolokitesvara prevalent in China) is spring, the embodiment of compassion and the motivation for manifesting in the world. Green Tara (from Tibetan Buddhism) is the summer, the manifestation of

compassion with one of her legs bent outward, into the world. Kali (from Hinduism) is the fall, the death-dealing one, who strips the world bare of illusion and the comfort of phenomena. Finally, winter is the woman who appears in Revelation 1:13. After the world of corruption has been destroyed, she arises as the resurrection of its perfection in a clear and radiant white light. This cycle of manifestation, understood as succeeding female forms, is but one possibility of role models. There are as many as we choose to see.

Feminism and Buddhism

Not Mixing Up Buddhism

Deborah Hopkinson

> Once a monk went to call on Mihu. On the way he met a woman living in a hut. The monk asked, "Do you have any disciples?" She said, "Yes." The monk asked, "Where are they?" She said, "The mountains, rivers and earth, the plants and trees, are all my disciples."
> The monk asked, "Are you a nun?" She said, "What do you see me as?" The monk said, "A layperson." She said, "You can't be a monk." The monk said, "You shouldn't mix up Buddhism." She said, "I'm not mixing up Buddhism." He said, "Aren't you mixing up Buddhism this way?" She said, "You're a man; I'm a woman. Where has there ever been any mixup?"

This wonderful story comes from T'ang Dynasty China and is part of a collection translated from various sources by the Chinese scholar Thomas Cleary. Like many Zen koans, it operates on more than one level. We may plumb its deepest meaning by using it as a meditation theme, and we may also reflect on its meaning and application for our everyday lives.

Very often in Zen koans, we find a monk struggling with basic existential questions. In this koan, the woman in a hut is continually challenging the wandering monk to question and throw away all his preconceived ideas and concepts—about Buddhism, about teachers and disciples, about laypeople and nuns. She cuts away his dependence on categories to prod him to find the place of no categories—the essential world of emptiness that is at the heart of Buddhist practice and human experience.

Very early in the dialogue the woman responds to the monk's attempt to place her as a student or a teacher by affirming that she has many disciples. "The mountains, rivers and earth, the plants and trees, are all my disciples." At one with the whole universe, she is teaching us that our essential self is no different from a blade of grass or a starving child. Dogen Zenji, the great teacher who brought Soto Zen to Japan in the 13th century, said, "Everything—blooming flowers, wild grasses, mountains, oceans, land, rivers—is the body and spirit of original Buddha mind. This original mind is a chair, a bamboo or a tree."

Yet it is clear that the monk cannot appreciate this response. "Are you a nun?" he asks, still trying to categorize. The woman gives him an opportunity to express or deepen his insight in this interaction by asking, "What do you see me as?" He replies, "A layperson." More categories!

"You can't be a monk!" she exclaims. Not only is she pointing out that a true monk is not caught up in fixed ideas about Buddhism, she is teaching and challenging him to come forth as his true self—completely empty, completely free, not bound by categories. This is freedom that is perfectly at home from moment to moment in the ordinary world of driving to work, making supper, and going to bed.

But the monk merely replies, "You shouldn't mix up Buddhism." We may share this defensiveness when our own self-image is threatened or challenged. If we strip away everything—our identity as a monk, a mother, a teacher, a lawyer, a lover—whatever—what is left?

"I'm not mixing up Buddhism," she asserts. Fundamentally, Buddhism is not about wearing robes, sitting cross-legged on cushions, or going on pilgrimage. "Aren't you mixing up Buddhism this way?" the monk asks. What is Buddhism, then, he finally questions. "You're a man; I'm a woman. Where has there ever been any mixup?" she responds.

When we experience the mountains and earth as our disciples we recognize that from the very beginning there is nothing to be mixed up at all. Dogen Zenji said, "The Buddha Way is intrinsically accomplished and perfect." We can see this all around us. This is the aspect of form, where trees are naturally tall and green, valleys are low, and men and women are uniquely different and individual. "You can't be a monk!" is the aspect of emptiness. In Zen practice we see for ourselves, moment to moment, how these are the same.

The story of the woman in a hut shows us how the essentials of Buddhism can be expressed, and it also holds particular significance as one of the most memorable stories of women in the Zen literature available to us. In a tradition where women role models are scarce, the woman in a hut shines as an extraordinary, though anonymous, teacher, whose example can guide us on our own path.

The woman in a hut urges the monk to develop a questioning spirit in order to discover the real meaning of Buddhism. This questioning spirit is at the heart of Zen—and feminism as well. What does it mean to be a woman? How can we rectify societal conditions of oppression and inequality? Who am I? What is the meaning of life and death? These are questions that inspire our spiritual searches and our political activities.

Zazen itself requires a scrupulous honesty, a questioning spirit with each breath. We do not sit cross-legged in meditation to plan the week's menus or solve a work problem. And true Zen practice calls for us to bring this questioning spirit and this honesty into all aspects of our lives.

For women, this has also meant infusing Buddhism with a feminist consciousness and working for a Western Buddhism that does not rely on any sexist categories or traditions but instead is true in all its aspects to the fact that men and women have been fundamentally equal from the beginning.

Feminists (both men and women) have worked in many areas within the newly transplanted religious practice. Many of the early translators of Japanese or Chinese Buddhist texts were not sensitive to sexist language. Pointing out that sexist language is inappropriate to Buddhist practice and helping to create new translations was one of the first areas in which changes were made.

Other changes have involved eliminating sex stereotyping in work and leadership roles, allowing both men and women to learn new skills and share skills in which they are already accomplished. Leadership roles, both within the meditation hall and in the governing of a Buddhist organization, have more and more reflected the increasing visibility of women in similar roles in the work world.

However, the implications of "not mixing up Buddhism" must go further than equal participation of men and women in Buddhist organizations. At the same time that women must assert their right to full participation, they must also continue to question the form and structure of Zen practice.

We must work to insure that we develop organizations which truly reflect the heart of Buddhism—the empty world of no male and no female that is simultaneously the ever-changing world of phenomena. How do we make our organization and practice open and accessible? How do we develop communities that recognize and delight in our individual differences—whether it be our sexual orientation, our age, our race, or our economic backgrounds? These are the kinds of questions we must begin to ask of ourselves and of our sanghas.

Developing a workable lay practice that is truly appropriate to the lives of contemporary women has, I believe, only just begun. If Buddhism and Buddhist teachers place their total emphasis on the importance of formal practice (attendance at retreats, completion of koans, hours of work contributed, etc.), women immersed in trying to juggle marriage, work, and children may find themselves isolated and discouraged. Their need for ways to continue their spiritual discipline must be recognized and incorporated into Buddhist teaching. Feminists must insure that Buddhist teachers continue to work with the vital issue of how to maintain Buddhist practice in everyday life. And they must bring back to the Buddhist center the insights learned by practicing in difficult and demanding everyday circumstances. Just as the woman in a hut rejects the monk's dependence upon the distinctions between lay and clerical, we must develop a Buddhism that is available and appropriate for everyone who desires to practice, whatever their circumstances.

On the level of practice, not mixing up Buddhism means wiping away the distinction between practitioner and non-practitioner, ordinary person and realized person. It means finding ways to practice when we cannot participate in formal practice, whether it be because of other commitments or because we are far from a teacher and other meditators. How do we practice when practice seems impossible? How can we discover the very essence of Zen in our daily lives though we may feel like failures as Zen students? How do we practice when we feel alone with our search for some other meaning in an increasingly intrusive, materialistic culture?

Zen practice is no guarantee or anything—perfection of character, peace, or happiness. Often we may feel, as T. S. Eliot expressed in the *Four Quartets*, "We are only undefeated because we have gone on trying."

And yet, ultimately, Zen can help us to know and appreciate each moment for what it is. After all, it is not so hard. An old Zen master once said, "Zazen is not difficult. It is a way that can lead you to your long lost home." That home, where Buddhism can never be mixed up, is right here.

Buddhism and Feminism; A Personal Synthesis

Rita M. Gross

For years, I have been seriously practicing Buddhism and feminism. Like other Western Buddhist women, I find each practice vital; I also find each enhances and complements the other. In a deep way, Buddhism and feminism share many essential insights. Each also contributes important insights and practices that the other needs to discover and utilize. I want to explore this interface of Buddhism and feminism further, focusing especially on the most basic similarities and differences between the two, and on how Buddhism supplements and goes beyond feminism.

To me, being a feminist simply means that one recognizes and acts on the fact that women are completely within the human realm rather than in some special category unto themselves. Feminism's double agenda is to open all human possibilities to all humans and to lift the stigma attached to women, women's work, and femaleness in so many cultures. In short, feminism promotes the essential dignity of women. I do not have in mind some kind of separatism or the idea that men or maleness are defective and the enemy. The emotional tone accompanying this brand of feminism is extremely unfortunate and hurts the cause immeasurably.

Defining what I am talking about as "Buddhism" is easier. I am not a professional Buddhologist and I am not talking about Buddhism speculatively or comprehensively. I will mainly confine myself to my experiences as a student of Chogyam Trungpa, Rinpoche, which affiliates me with the Karma Kagyu lineage of Tibetan Vajrayana Buddhism.

Buddhism and feminism are not usually paired. Most people with active feminist concerns know almost nothing about Buddhism and assume it fits the general patriarchal mold. A few well-known statements, such as the relative misfortune of a female birth vis-a-vis a male, the vinaya (monastic) rules ranking all nuns below any monk regardless of seniority or spiritual attainment, and the infamous comment that the dharma (truth or teaching) would decline twice as quickly because women had been permitted to enter monastic life, bolster such assumptions about the inherently patriarchal cast. Furthermore, some Western Buddhist women, who once called themselves feminists, have left self-conscious identification with feminism behind, claiming feminism is too ideologically egocentric to be compatible with Buddhadharma. Sometimes there seems to be little acknowledgement of anything feminist, even among Buddhists who embody and demand within their own sangha the best insights of feminism.

Nevertheless, especially for one who is deeply involved in both practices, there are basic and important insights shared by Buddhism and feminism.

First, contrary to most of Western philosophical and theological heritage, both Buddhism and feminism begin with experience, stress experiential understanding enormously, and move from experience to theory.

Regarding Buddhism, this starting point is so basic it hardly needs to be demonstrated. It is the reason for the continual emphasis on sitting meditation as the only basis for study and philosophy. This basic point is borne out by countless statements in Buddhist literature from earliest scriptures to the present.

Feminist theology has its origins in the gut feeling that what we were taught about our religious tradition simply did not mesh with what women experienced. Therefore, the basic practices in feminist theology are to rest with that discontinuity, to explore experience, and to come up with language that conforms with experience, rather than pays lip service to received tradition.

Allegiance to experience before theory leads to a second important similarity between Buddhism and feminism: the will and courage to go against the grain at any cost, to hold to insights of truth, no matter how bizarre they seem from a conventional point of view.

This similar willingness to hold to basic experience rather than conventionality is connected with a third similarity between Buddhism and feminism. Both use their courage and experiential base to explore how mind operates. Buddhism explores the patterns of ego and the nature of egoless being. It explores the nature of ego-ful, problematic experience and also the egoless, non-grasping, basic state of mind. Feminism, on the other hand, explores an aspect of ego—sexual identity and the way in which it determines or prohibits societal or psychic access to various experiences and privileges—in a completely thoroughgoing fashion. Thus, both explore how habitual ego patterns block well-being. This is the most profound similarity between feminism and Buddhism.

However, in the exploration of ego, Buddhism and feminism also differ significantly. Buddhism explores patterns of ego or territoriality, pain and clinging. It also teaches the path to transcend ego. Buddhism is significantly and dramatically more developed in this sense of path and discipline than is feminism. Furthermore, its presentation of egolessness is beyond anything feminism, or most other value systems, have yet envisioned.

On the other hand, in its exploration of one of the fundamental habitual patterns of ego—the territoriality and sense of limitation and/or privilege that are part of sexual identity in conventional people—feminism has laid bare a dimension of ego that Buddhism seems not to have noticed. To me, this aspect of feminist thought is among its most applicable and relevant contributions. The acknowledgment and exploration of gender-based ego-patterns show how they arise from societal patterns and pressures, and how critically and massively they can affect one's psychology and one's sense of the environment.

Buddhism rarely asks why its institutions make it easier for men to pursue the spiritual disciplines leading to egolessness. It has not dealt with the contradiction that sometimes masters advanced in their development went along with conventional stereotypes, fears, hostilities and restrictions concerning women. To be able to see at last these perversions of sexual identity as a dimension of ego, to see them as another trick of grasping and territoriality standing in the way of egolessness, would be an auspicious result of the meeting between feminism and Buddhism.

Buddhism provides something feminism does not in the depth it goes to lay bare the basic human situation. The ground for development is the practice of mindfulness meditation. This ground does not depend on being a Buddhist, but on discipline and openness. The sense of dawning egolessness resulting from this practice manifests as an ever-increasing gentleness, softness and openness which has nothing to do with being weak, powerless or submissive. In fact, if anything, a sense of dignity, strength and invulnerability, in the positive sense, grows with the increasing gentleness and softness. This gentling process has implications for feminist theory and practice.

The understanding that suffering is basic, the first noble truth of Buddhism, brings with it some relaxation from the constant struggle to avoid pain. As I understood this I became dissatisfied with feminism's more superficial discussion of suffering. Feminist theology has never distinguished between avoidable pain caused by patriarchal, sexist values and institutions and the basic pain of being human, nor has it ever considered the inevitability of suffering, no matter how perfect social arrangements may be. While eradicating patriarchy and the suffering it causes remains an important priority, it is clear such an agenda is naive if it is the only method for understanding and dealing with suffering.

Because feminism has no avenue of approach to basic pain, much feminist theory and practice has a kind of frantic quality. An understanding of suffering would offer individual feminists a quality of peacefulness and the means to work on problems without alienating everyone in the process.

These thoughts about the pervasive quality of pain lead to another way feminism is softened by Buddhism. In my experience, the practice of mindfulness-awareness meditation is the most useful technique for working with and transforming anger that I have encountered. It invites one to acknowledge rather than to ignore all facets of one's experience. Then it gradually, slowly allows one to tap into, transform, and use the energy of anger and aggression in more enlightened ways. Since anger is such a basic dimension of feminist experience, I want to explore further the experience of anger and possibilities of exhausting anger, then using its energy.

First one experiences anger as one's consciousness is raised about the degraded ways in which women have been treated. Then, eventually, something else must happen. Anger can either be indulged or exhausted. Feminists who make a career of expressing anger obviously indulge it, and by conventional logic they could make a strong case. Everywhere one turns, constant advertisements, news stories, and insensitive language irritate one's consciousness. Isn't it important to keep those feelings going? Isn't the anger righteous and doesn't one have a right to such feelings? Even if one doesn't identify with feminists' anger, I suspect everyone experiences some private emotionalism about which they feel such possessiveness and self-righteousness.

In the choice between repressing or expressing such emotionalism, much can be said about the healthier ability to experience and perhaps express the emotion. That is why all schools of feminist theology value anger as part of the process of growth. But Buddhist practice works to take one beyond both repression and expression to the point where teachings about being without passion and without aggression begin to make sense. Then one begins to see how cumbersome and counter-productive all that emotionalism can be.

Anger becomes cumbersome in that it is quite enervating and painful to experience. Outbursts of anger, or the refined and precise knife-thrusts of analytic anti-sexist rhetoric, bring temporary relief but do not satisfy for long. Then the cycle starts again, but the process doesn't produce much sense of well-being. There is no need to trot out the whole repertoire of emotional responses when one sees what is going on. Instead, one can, with gentleness and humor, recognize the process.

Dependent on the world for a sense of well-being, one is caught up forever in the throes of resentment. But if one deals with the totality of one's world without projection or aggression, no matter how uncomfortable that may be, all situations are experienced as learning environments and no resentment, or egoistic reaction, is added to the experience.

Anger-filled reactions begin to seem like a luxury because one knows they have more to do with indulging one's own sense of injury than dealing with the problem. Demonstrating personal anger polarizes and hardens the opposition; it rarely changes situations or people's minds. In contrast, people are so surprised by gentleness that often the results are unexpectedly positive.

In general, the effect of practice is that one becomes less ideological, less tied to rigidly held fixed beliefs. It is somewhat of a shock to discover how problematic ideology is, how aggressive it can be, and how it provides a closed, comfortable identity. Ideology is a protective shell preserving one from immediate contact with situations. Feminism can and has functioned as such for some of its adherents.

However, it is important to notice that as ideology becomes less viable the result is not a supine acceptance of the status quo. Feminists fear that without a strong ideological commitment to feminism they would be left acquiescing to sexism. A middle way is in order. This non-dualistic, non-fixated allegiance to "neither this nor that" seems the hardest aspect of Indian spirituality to teach Westerners, and also the hardest to grasp. But it seems the only way to maneuver between the ideology of the radical and the conventional.

Thus my own involvement with Buddhist practice has led me to several insights about feminism I would not otherwise have made, insights which strengthen and deepen my feminism. Basic mindfulness practice does not necessitate giving up or adding specific rituals and beliefs. Mindfulness practice can be independent of its Buddhist moorings and some groups are actively working to develop formats to teach mindfulness practice in a secular manner and context. Most Buddhists feel that mindfulness practice itself is of value to anyone, without regard to their affiliation or lack of affiliation with a particular religious institution or teachings. I am no exception. If the next development in feminist theology were for practitioners to become seriously committed to basic mindfulness practice, the results would be extraordinary.

Sexual Power Abuse: Neglect and Misuse of a Buddhist Precept

Carla Brennan

Buddhism, in its move to the West, has found itself in a new and different culture. Unlike Asia, the West is sexually permissive with few mores to regulate and govern sexual behavior. We are no longer confined to strict sex roles, and activities are no longer sex segregated. Women participate with men in all areas of life. This means that social, professional and sexual relationships between men and women are quite different from the Eastern cultures in which Buddhism arose. In addition, the dramatic changes in sexual behavior and in women's roles in the last 20 years have resulted in tension and confusion about sexuality within our own culture.

In all Buddhist traditions, the third precept speaks to sexual misconduct. For nuns and monks it is a precept of celibacy; for laypeople it is a precept against the misuse of sexual relations. Although the interpretation and application of this precept has varied, the essential message has remained the same. One Buddhist meditation teacher explains that this precept:

> ... speaks of refraining from adultery, from sexual relations with those not free and from sexual relations through coercion. To honor this precept means refraining from acting sexually in any way that brings harm to any other being.[1]

The third precept is not an arbitrary commandment that one must obey to be a "good" Buddhist, rather it is common sense advice alerting us to the delicate and potentially volatile nature of sexual relations. Simply put, people can easily misuse sexual activity and bring suffering to themselves and others. The third precept, needed now more than ever to help us wisely adjust to changes in sexual mores, has been ignored or misinterpreted within many Buddhist communities in the West.

Numerous cases of spiritual teachers (some married and others supposedly celibate) initiating sex with students have become common knowledge. I have been close to the source of some incidents and distant from others and I cannot verify all the specific details or information. However, even a conservative estimate would show this behavior to be widespread. Certainly not every instance of sexual relations between teachers and students constitutes sexual misconduct. It is understandable that a single, non-celibate teacher might become involved with a student. It is the motivation behind the sexual act that determines whether the precept has been broken. Is the sexual activity a genuine expression of love, intimacy, and connection to another human being or is it an expression of power and an attempt to exploit another person to satisfy one's desires? Although many people are uncomfortable with the sexual behavior of some teachers and students, there has been considerable reluctance to speak out publicly against this activity. This silence may come from self-doubt, deference to a teacher, or fear of being ignored, ridiculed, or ostracized. Some people may fear that the controversy will threaten the continuation of their community. Investigating incidents of sexual abuse can unearth painful and angry feelings.

My own experience of sexual harassment from a spiritual teacher may help explain the complexity of feelings involved. Although my experience was mild compared to many other women's, it shows how these situations may develop and indicates the effect they can have.

My first and only encounter with this Zen teacher was during a seven-day retreat. After the second or third day he began to touch and hug me during the frequent interviews. At first this contact seemed casual and friendly and helped me feel welcome in a strange environment. However, he became more aggressive. I soon realized that his actions were motivated by sexual desire and not by concern for me.

I became confused and embarrassed; I began to worry about what he might do next. The touching felt intrusive and disrespectful. However, I found it difficult to effectively rebuff his advances. I was afraid he would not listen and would accuse me of making a mountain out of a molehill. I didn't want to make a scene, possibly "ruining" the retreat and alienating the teacher. I felt vulnerable and alone. I responded by being timidly discouraging; his efforts began to subside and the retreat soon ended.

Afterward I was angry with myself for feeling intimidated and for not responding more assertively. I was angry at the teacher for imposing his desires on me and using his position as a teacher to indirectly elicit subtle sexual contact. He was diverting time and energy away from the purpose of the interview. Most importantly, he was relating to me, a woman, as a sexual object rather than as a serious Zen student. I have not returned to study with this teacher and I have vowed to express loudly and clearly my disapproval if I should have a similar experience. Although this situation was more annoying than traumatizing, it made clear to me how potentially painful sexual harassment can be and how it can interfere with one's practice.

Sexual harassment is broadly defined as "unwelcome sexual advances, requests for sexual favors, and other verbal or physical conduct of a sexual nature"[2] that is offensive or intimidating and interferes with one's working, learning, or living situations. Although the literature quoted below discussed sexual harassment on the job and at school, it is easy to apply these definitions to our life within spiritual communities. A brochure published by the University of Massachusetts, where I have worked and studied sexual abuse, says that:

> Sexual harassment is a form of discrimination because it unjustly deprives a person of equal treatment...Sexual harassment is primarily directed at women by men in positions of power...It embraces a wide spectrum of conduct which may include:
>
> —...looks, leering, gestures, jokes, innuendoes, sexual slurs, comments, or epithets of a sexual nature.
>
> —Subtle pressure for sexual activity.
>
> —Sexual remarks about a person's clothing, body, or sexual activity.
>
> —Unnecessary touching, in any form.
>
> —Demanding sexual favors, accompanied by implied or overt threats concerning one's job, grades, letters of recommendation, etc.[3]

The pamphlet also says that:

> A person in a position of power is in a position to coerce, whether knowingly or not, those who rely on them for supervision, guidance, and academic and career support. Sexual attention is coercive and destructive to one who does not feel free to say no, and is always suspect when coming from a person in a position of more power, authority or control.[4]

It is clear that sexual harassment is fundamentally an issue of power. Women are usually the targets and victims, however, it is certainly possible that men may be victims of other men or women, and that women may be the victims of other women.

In sexual harassment, "as in rape and sexual assault, the assertion of power and dominance...are often more important than the sexual interaction itself."[5] The majority of business executives surveyed on sexual harassment "correlate the perceived seriousness of the behavior with the power of the person making the advance."[6]

Power is the ability to control, manipulate and influence one's environment, both in terms of people and material objects. Experiencing and expressing power is a part of being alive; a powerful person can work toward harmony or toward disruption. Unchecked power that does not receive feedback or criticism, however, often becomes distorted and self-serving. People involved in power abuses lose perspective, cease to feel accountable for their behavior, and become blind to their real motivations and to the harmful consequences of their actions.

Sexual harassment is illegal under Title VII of the Civil Rights Act of 1964. An official at the Massachusetts Commission Against Discrimination said that there are few court cases regarding sexual harassment in religious organizations. He did feel, however, that there are grounds for a legal suit in some cases. Hopefully, situations of sexual misconduct can be resolved from within the community rather than in a court of law. However, stronger measures may need to be taken to curb this behavior, protect students, and afford women equal treatment. It is important to understand that sexual harassment is taken very seriously in the secular world and that spiritual teachers are not above the law.

Spiritual teachers are often accorded an unusual amount of uncontested political power within their community. The hierarchical organizational structures adopted from the East often give the head teacher the final say on all decisions, no matter how important or petty, practice related or worldly, or how qualified the teacher may be to advise. Systems of peer supervision, accountability, and grievance procedures may not be adequate.

These hierarchical forms reflect the values of the feudal systems of class division and authoritarian control of the societies where most Buddhist traditions developed, rather than the modern values of democracy, equality, and individual responsibility.

Katy Butler, in discussing the San Francisco Zen Center, explains:

> For a long time, most of us accepted without thinking it through,

> foreign conceptions of hierarchy, of information restricted on a "need to know" basis. Coming from a culture almost devoid of ways of showing respect, some of us hungrily took on another way. Now these foreign ideas are being tested for their usefulness against the genius of Western culture: democracy, open information, a free press, psychological development, the separation of Church and State, and a system of checks and balances.[7]

The organizational structures handed down to us from the East are not sacred; there is nothing more "spiritual" about one organizational form over another. However, the structure should be appropriate to the time and place, reflect the values and vision of the group, and serve the needs of the members. Since power abuses as well as related problems are re-occurring in spiritual communities, we need to question seriously the effectiveness of strict hierarchical forms and begin to investigate alternatives.

The "myth of infallibility"[8] is another source of power for spiritual teachers. This is the belief that teachers always act, think or feel from an "enlightened" state and are therefore always right. Often when students do not approve of what a teacher is doing, they blame themselves for not having enough wisdom to understand the teacher. This belief gives spiritual teachers nearly unlimited authority, and such power may be very attractive. Although a teacher may be put on a pedestal of perfection, he (or she) may have less than ideal desires and act in less than ideal ways. In order to maintain and protect this powerful false image a teacher may decide, consciously or unconsciously, to deny or hide his acts. Other members of the sangha who rely psychologically on the ideal image of a teacher may aid in the deception. However, as Santayana says, "There is, indeed, no idol ever identified with the ideal which honest experience, even without cynicism, will not someday, unmask and discredit."[9]

The notion that a teacher exemplifies perfection betrays a fundamental misconception about practice and enlightenment. Spiritual growth is not attaining a permanent perfected state that is rid of negative emotions or experiences. It is, instead, finding out who we are. Awareness and acceptance of all parts of ourselves grants us freedom and enables us to understand and have compassion for others.

In spite of the obvious power a spiritual teacher may have over a student, sexual abuse would not continue if women (and men) clearly recognized these situations for what they were, spoke openly, and refused to participate. The reasons why women get involved in unhealthy sexual relationships with spiritual teachers are many. The relationship between a teacher and student is usually personal and intimate, more so than relationships usually found in the workplace and at universities. Many of us have deep needs for love and acceptance from those who are important to us. Sexual contact may seem like the only way to get special attention from a teacher. A woman may feel that she has fallen in love with a teacher and she may misinterpret his sexual interest as the reciprocation of her feelings. Women have also been conditioned to get their feelings of self-worth and status from men; sexual involvement with a teacher may give a woman the feeling of validation, importance, and power that she cannot give herself.

Women may also try to satisfy power needs through sexual manipulation. Seduction of a teacher may bring the satisfaction of conquest and control. Women may also, consciously or unconsciously, try to climb the sangha's "corporate ladder" by offering sexual favors.

Dependency on a practice, community, or teacher creates a state of powerlessness that makes a woman very susceptible to sexual power abuse. This dependency has many sources. Joining a spiritual community may fulfill strong needs for family, security, and identity. Community living can be a refuge from the burdens, responsibilities, and problems of daily life. People can cling to a spiritual path as the hope for an end to years of pain and despair, and practice can bring meaning into an empty life. A woman may surrender to the sexual demands of the spiritual teacher out of fear of losing this support.

To consciously stop this cycle of abuse, we, as women, need to explore our illusions of teachers and practice, our dependency needs, and our unconscious actions that create pain for ourselves by stepping out of patterns that perpetuate sexual abuse, while at the same time, confronting teachers on their sexual misconduct. We need to replace complicity with truth.

We live in a world where sexual and physical abuse of women is part of our "normal" existence. Rape, sexual abuse of children, wife battering and pornography have touched many women's lives. As one researcher on sexual harassment says, "the intimate violation of women by men is sufficiently pervasive in American society as to be nearly invisible."[10] It is as if we have lived with the foul smell of abuse for so long that we cannot always perceive it.

The serious self-examination that is taking place in several Buddhist communities in the West is helping to heal the damage that has been done, and to bring to light the issue of sexual misconduct. Feminist awareness is growing within American Buddhism, and women are talking openly and honestly about what has been happening. As we begin to look clearly at sexual misconduct, we can return to the third precept to explore its meaning, and to reaffirm its value in a new time and place. And by doing so, we will reach a deeper, more fulfilling, and mature relationship with ourselves, with our practice, and with the world around us.

[1]Jack Kornfield, "Sex Lives of the Gurus," Yoga Journal, Issue 63, July/August 1985, p. 66.
[2]Federal Register, *Rules and Regulations* (Washington, D.C.:Equal Employment Opportunity Commission's Final Amendment to Guidelines on Discrimination Because of Sex, 29 CFR Part 1604, November, 1980) Vol. 45 No. 219.
[3]University of Massachusetts at Amherst, "Sexual Harassment—The Problem, The Policy, and The Procedures" (Amherst, MA:1983).
[4]Ibid.
[5]James C. Renick, "Sexual Harassment at Work: Why It Happens," *Personnel Journal*, 1980, p. 658.
[6]Eliza C. G. Collins and Timothy B. Blodgett, "Some See It... Some Won't," *Harvard Business Review*, March-April, 1981. p. 77.
[7]Katy Butler, "Events are the Teacher," *CoEvolutionary Quarterly*, Winter 1983, p. 123.
[8]Deborah Hopkinson, "Not Mixing Up Buddhism," *Kahawai*, Vol. VI, No. 1, Winter 1984, p. 7.
[9]George Santayana, *Little Essays* (Ed. Smith Constable) p. 41.
[10]Renick, p. 658.

Issues in Everyday Life

Ordinary Practice

Fran Tribe

Combining "serious" Zen practice with domestic life might have been considered impossible or even absurd two or three hundred years ago, especially for women. But the same social and technological conditions which now make it possible for women to combine having a career with having a family, make the combination of practice and family life possible for us. Not only possible but desirable. Practice and domestic life can enrich each other and enable us to integrate diverse parts of ourselves. Together they ground us in what is fundamental about being human. Suzuki Roshi said we practice Zen to become who we really are. For many of us, this process includes being householders and parents.

Buddha started a tradition of leaving home to follow the spiritual path, but it is not necessary to be literally homeless in order to practice. Nor is it necessary to be literally destitute to learn non-attachment. Homelessness is a state of mind, a questioning, a deep realization that there is no place to rest or to hide. And a monk can be as attached to his robe, his bowl, and his poverty as a rich person to his countless possessions. We shouldn't confuse sincere practice with some particular lifestyle.

Actually, monastic life and domestic life are not so different. Monks and housewives face similar problems and opportunities. Both are committed to putting the well-being of others above their own. Both have demanding daily schedules which typically include a lot of repetitious work such as cleaning, cooking, etc. And both monks and housewives are outside the mainstream of society, although they are supported by it (financially and otherwise). The monk's schedule and duties are set by his monastery or temple, but a housewife must create her own order, her own priorities, and her own schedule. In doing this, she can make her home a peaceful island in a chaotic world.

People go to monasteries to be refreshed in some deep way, and it is traditional for monks to share their practice with guests. Often students will say that when they first began coming to their meditation center they felt as if they had finally come home or found their true home. But the center itself need not be physically our home. The feeling of coming home is the awakening of the way-seeking mind; a glimpse of our true nature. We can find ways to make our private homes nourish our true nature and inspire or refresh our own families and guests. This is one of the challenges of lay practice. And when we rise to meet it, our true home is everywhere, and all our activities reflect our true nature.

"When your practice is calm and ordinary," Suzuki Roshi said, "everyday life itself is enlightment." He stressed this point over and over again in many ways, and his teaching can be particularly encouraging for people who are trying to take care of homes, jobs, relationships, and children. But it can be difficult to let go of our preconceptions about what practice should look like. We think that a monk working in the temple garden is practicing, but it is harder to see that a lay person taking care of her or his own garden may be practicing, too. True practice does not live in any institution; it lives in the innermost part of each of us.

When we go to sit at the zendo, we don't just walk in and sit down on a cushion. We bow as we enter the room. We bow to our cushion. We bow away from it. When we get up, we fluff our cushion; we bow to it. We bow to the people we are sitting with, to Buddha, to our teacher. In the zendo, our bowing is taking care of everything. It is taking nothing for granted. Outside the zendo, we may not actually bow to everything, but our interaction with things and with people can have this quality of gassho. It depends only on our sincerity. When we are completely sincere in our effort to see and accept things as they are, all our activities are practice.

We often talk about practice and everyday life as opposites. We feel that zazen is "pure" practice, while work or everyday life is "applied" practice. And in both spiritual and scientific circles, the "pure" activity is more prestigious than the applied side of it. When we think this way, we are cutting off the possibility of our everyday life inspiring our meditation practice. We assume it has to be the other way around. This kind of thinking can turn the Bodhisattva path into a narrow, one-way street.

It is easy to fall into the materialistic trap of thinking that zazen is some kind of answer to all of life's problems. If we sit regularly, making great effort, we feel this should be reflected in our everyday life. We tend to feel that if our zazen is good, the surface of our life will naturally become smooth, free from flaws, and shiny like a well-finished table. This is our American Zen version of the old Puritan ethic: virtue is rewarded. If we sit for a long time and still our life is flawed (or heaven forbid, a mess), we may feel that we have failed: "I just got it wrong, I never learned to sit properly." Judging our practice in this way can lead to great discouragement. We need to pay attention to our life from moment to moment, just as we pay attention to our breath in zazen. Making judgments is something extra. There is a voice deep inside each of us telling us where to go, but we often can't hear it through the "should" and "shouldn't" our mind bombards us with.

Putting one foot in front of the other, trusting we will find the way, we find that everyday life is just pure activity. One effort. One mind. Just this mop on the floor, just this sucking baby, just this screaming baby—just this, just this—now. Any lifestyle or set of circumstances can be our training ground.

Suzuki Roshi was my first teacher, and I have had the great good fortune to be able to work with other fine Zen teachers. But I have to admit that I have learned more from my children than from any of them. When my first was just a newborn, he opened my eyes to the meaning of practice. Just going to Joshua when he cried, just cleaning up his messes, moving from one thing to another, I experienced being present in each moment. "This is beginner's mind," I said to myself. For the first time I understood what Suzuki Roshi had been talking about. "This is sesshin," I felt, as the days and nights grew longer and harder. My children are like little teachers crying "Attention! Attention!" They are constantly bringing me back to this moment.

I had been sitting for seven years before my first child was born. The years before his birth I did little zazen, but the year before that I spent at Tassajara (San Francisco Zen Center's training monastery). I was struck by how similar my year at Tassajara and my first few years of mothering felt, but I assumed that the monastery was where practice really took place. I assumed that my feeling that what I was doing with my child was practice must be some kind of misunderstanding. My doubt and confusion grew.

For many years, taking care of my family was my main activity. The question: how can this be practice? was seldom out of my mind. I did not bring it up purposely to remind myself of my commitment to Zen; it was just there in the background of everything I did. It was my koan. There were times when I found myself bowing a lot or inventing small rituals to begin, end, or tie together my day. Sometimes, when Joshua cried a lot, I found that chanting calmed us both. I structured my time carefully and took care of household chores with great attention, as if the Buddha himself were coming to dinner. For months I did not sit zazen or go near a zendo. The months became years. Sometimes I felt that I "should be sitting" and I'd sit a few mornings and quit again. It felt good to sit, but zazen aroused my feelings of being isolated and alienated from the world of "real practice," the world where people got up early every morning without fail, sat sesshins, and kept both worldly and domestic involvements to a minimum.

During the years that I lived this way, caring for my family and the place where I was living, doing some ceramics and yoga, I was alone much of the time. I had few friends. My husband was a psychiatric resident for the first four years of my housewife phase, and he was not home much. He was having his own difficult times. We both felt confused and discouraged about practice.

At some level I knew I was practicing sincerely and intensely, but I was afraid to believe it because I looked just like any other housewife, not at all like a Zen student. I felt that Zen had brought me to a point of understanding my deep desire to raise a family and dropped me there. I missed my sangha, but felt no one would understand me in the world of "real practice." I knew I could not go back to a community whose primary commitment was to a strict schedule of zazen, study, and work.

In the bigger world, having babies and being a housewife were suspect for other reasons. The women's movement at that time (1974) attacked traditionally female activities as counter-revolutionary, reactionary, or just plain stupid. It surprised me to find so little social support for even the conventional side of my life. I had many doubts. Was I crazy? Were the feminists crazy? I had always had doubts about my practice. Sitting for years was not supposed to lead you to find you were a mother at heart. If I were truly committed to practice, wouldn't I be looking for babysitters and beating a path to the nearest Zen center?

It felt very right taking care of home and family; I could tell it was coming from the deepest part of me. But I feared this proved I was, deep down, really not Zen student material after all. A fraud, a dilettante, just not good enough. Maybe everyone was originally enlightened except me.

Looking back on this time, I feel that I had tuned into an ancient practice, the way one might tune in a far-away radio station. For millenia women have been taking care of babies and homes, gardens, and whatever else needed care. They worked with great care and concentration; indeed, their lives depended on it. This is practicing "as if to save your head from fire." They invented rituals to give rhythm to their work and to appease the fearful forces which controlled life and death. They were constantly aware of impermanence because death was always close at hand. Husbands went hunting and did not return. More babies died than lived. More mothers, too. This was everyday life and ultimate reality.

I don't personally know anyone who died in childbirth or had a baby who died in infancy. This is a quirk of time and circumstance. For centuries women rubbed noses with death daily; in most of the world, this is still true. We are no different than these women. And in that vulnerable time after we give birth, we can connect with the fundamental process of life and death. It is a priceless practice opportunity.

Even though we can expect to survive childbirth, even though we can choose not to bear children, we are no different than women who had no choice but to confront life and death in that way. In addition we have the opportunity to practice Buddhism and to become who we really are in its full sense. The options we have today are unique in history. Although we have more options than our grandmothers and our sisters who live in less fortunate circumstances, fundamental reality is the same for all of us. Tending our children, our garden, or whatever, with no thought of past or future, we can experience oneness as surely as a monk or nun who sits facing a wall. It depends only on our sincerity. The dharma gate is open to everyone.

Parentbirth

Teresa Vast

The most succinct statement about the birth of my child came in a note from a friend: "Congratulations, Angela, for dwelling nowhere and coming forth." Even after months of anticipation, her arrival was like something out of a magic show. As I watched her emerge from my body, complete and separate, I had the strong sense of her coming into being from nothingness. And just as she came forth from nowhere, simultaneously I emerged from nowhere as a parent. It is my experience of parentbirth, that is, the transformation of a non-parent to a parent, that I wish to explore here.

For years I couldn't imagine being a parent. Many questions arose about what parenthood would be for me. There were also concerns that a child would interfere with formal Zen training and would limit my participation in many other activities. Because of these questions and concerns, I concluded that I must not be ready to have a child.

I felt limited by my definitions of Zen practice, which basically consisted of my experiences in a formal setting—first as a single person and then as a married person without children. With no models of a successful combination of parenthood with formal Zen practice, I could not fathom how my practice could continue with a child, and I was afraid to give up that which had been most precious to me.

Yet in spite of my concerns about continuing my activities, I felt a growing desire to start a family. After years of working with young children and their families, I had become fascinated by the intimacy of sharing in the life of a child, and I felt drawn more and more to nurturing a child of my own.

Gradually, over a period of time, my concerns diminished and I discovered an openness to practicing within the context of parenthood, and a willingness to include a new being in my life. The barriers I had imagined lost their solidity and instead I could view my concerns as problems with which to work.

But even with pregnancy, my questions continued: What is a mother? How will I be as a parent? I could never answer these to my satisfaction. Then, with Angela's birth, the questions fell away. As suddenly as she was born, I became a parent, and now there is nothing more natural than parenting. I am still the person I have been, yet I am a parent at the same time.

Actually, to say that I transformed from non-parent to parent is not quite accurate. Although one might say that there are nine months of becoming, I had no experience of "becoming" a parent. There is a passage in Dogen Zenji's essay, "Genjokoan," which elucidates this point:

> Firewood turns into ash, and does not turn into firewood again. But do not suppose that the ash is after and the firewood is before. We must realize that firewood is in the state of being firewood, and it has its before and after. Yet despite this past and future, its present is independent of them. Ash is in the state of being ash, and it has its before and after. Just as firewood does not become firewood again after it is ash, so after one's death one does not return to life again. Thus, that life does not become death is an unqualified fact of the Buddha Dharma; for this reason, life is called the non-born. That death does not become life is the Buddha's revolving of the confirmed Dharma wheel; therefore death is called the non-extinguished. Life is a period of itself. Death is a period of itself. For example, they are like winter and spring. We do not think that winter becomes spring, nor do we say that spring becomes winter.

Being a non-parent is a period of itself and being a parent is a period of itself. There is no "becoming" which connects the two. Undeniably there is a before and after of parenthood. Yet within the activities of parenting, each moment of being a parent is beyond before and after. There is only being with this baby in this very moment.

During the past few months I have been asked countless times, "How do you like being a mother?" Each time I have been stuck for an answer, because, though I am definitely "mothering," I had not identified myself with the label "mother." There is just nursing, changing this diaper, playing this game, laughing together. "Being a mother" describes the context of my activity, but does not touch the content of my experience. I am simply being myself with this child.

Admittedly, it has been difficult to maintain my daily sitting practice since Angela's birth. Most days it has been impossible—fifteen minutes while she naps, a few moments while nursing, ten minutes before collapsing into bed. However, I have not responded to this situation in any way I would have predicted. I had assumed I might feel regret, if not resentment. Instead, I appreciate all the more those moments of zazen that are available to me.

What is most striking to me in all of this is the contrast between thinking about being a parent and the actual experience of being a parent. It is the same with our practice: attempts to conceptualize it fail to bring the experience of it any closer. As a beginning Zen student I believed that, once enlightened, I would be magically different. But both in practice and in parenthood I find that I simply become more of who I already am. From a distance, being a parent seemed different from being myself. But with parentbirth, the experience was completely ordinary—was there ever a time without this child? Was I ever not a parent?

Woman to Child
Judith Wright

You who were darkness warmed my flesh
where out of darkness rose the seed.
Then all a world I made in me;
all the world you hear and see
hung upon my dreaming blood.

There moved the multitudinous stars,
and coloured birds and fishes moved.
There swam the sliding continents.
All time lay rolled in me, and sense,
and love that knew not its beloved.

O node and focus of the world,
I hold you deep within that well
you shall escape and not escape -
that mirrors still your sleeping shape,
that nurtures still your crescent cell.

I wither and you break from me;
yet though you dance in living light
I am the earth, I am the root,
I am the stem that fed the fruit,
the link that joins you to the night.

On Abortion

Margot Wallach Milliken

I. 1980

Abortion is a difficult subject to write about. Even among friends it is not usually discussed. It surprises me how many women have never shared their abortion experiences with others. Whatever the reasons—guilt, sorrow, anger, a lack of understanding or perspective—this silence keeps abortion mysterious and unapproachable. I'm not sure the mystery is ever understood, but the silence can be broken.

I first got pregnant at age 21. I had no question about what to do. I arranged for an abortion without even discussing it with the man involved. I did not allow myself to feel fear or sadness, or to consider the moral questions involved. I looked at abortion as just a medical procedure, and afterwards I was relieved to have gotten myself out of a difficult situation.

When I was 24, I got pregnant a second time. In the intervening years, however, I had explored various spiritual paths, finally choosing Buddhist meditation. I was particularly attracted by the Buddha's teaching of respect and care for all things in the universe. Now I saw abortion as killing. I was full of guilt, terrified of making a conscious decision to end life. I alternately felt self-pity at being the victim of an ill-fitted diaphragm, and anger that both the doctor and I were so stupid and inept.

I did not want the baby. My relationship with the man involved was falling apart, and my financial resources were limited. Most importantly, I didn't want the responsibility of a child.

At some point, though, I became aware of the miracle of conception and the extraordinary experience of holding a new life in my body.

This is so subtle and wondrous I have no words to describe the feeling. I didn't want to deny this life force.

My mood swings were tremendous. No laws, morals, or theories could help me make the decision of whether or not to abort the child. It had to come from within. I was upset by my lack of clarity about what I wanted and by the way I had let my sexuality undermine the rest of my life.

A wise friend encouraged me to love this new being, accept it for what it was, send it loving thoughts, and if I decided to have the abortion, to also wish the being a peaceful journey. The other advice was to send myself healing and loving thoughts, and to be completely accepting of the many reactions and feelings I was experiencing. Finally I reached a point of balance and understanding.

I had the abortion, and now, four years later, I still have questions. My questions are not about whether or not I did the right thing; I'm sure I did. My questions are about the society we live in, where single parents are isolated and women are largely responsible for child-rearing, often without supportive communities or relationships. Why are women the ones who must deal with the children that result from unplanned pregnancies?

My other questions are more personal. Do I have the right to make a decision to end a life? If I was poor or had several children already, the answer might be clearer. If I had had no choice, I know I would have cared for and loved my child. Was the fact that I was not "ready" for motherhood enough of a justification? It seems a little strange to me, this power we have to say yes or no to these new lives.

There is also the place in me where I see life and death continuing and changing from one form to another. To call life good and death bad is a distinction that ultimately, I feel, is not correct. And then there is the mystery of carrying a new life in one's body. Only a woman can know how that feels and still choose to end that life. That part is not resolved for me.

II. 1986

Six years have passed since I wrote this piece for *Kahawai*. Nine months have passed since the birth of my first child. I felt healthy, energetic, and full of life when I was pregnant. My labor was uncomplicated and straightforward. I squatted, moaned, and pushed my son out into the world. As I watched him take his first breath and cry his first cry, I knew I had seen a miracle. I felt exhausted and ecstatic.

This all stands in sharp contrast to the wrenching pain I, and others

I have spoken with, experienced at the time of our abortions. Making that choice is one of the most difficult in a woman's life.

Given the present political and social climate, we are in danger of losing the legal right to choose abortion. While I do not believe abortion is something that should be legislated against, I do feel it is an option that should not be taken lightly. Even if it seems that the best choice is to terminate a pregnancy, we must acknowledge we are ending a potential life. This seems more honest than acting as if our "pro-choice" stance does not involve taking life, even though we may assume that that life is not fully realized, conscious, or developed.

In the past few years I have learned to feel more accepting of my body and my feelings. I rejoice in my sexuality and in being a woman. Since becoming a mother, life is more precious to me and also seems more fragile. I feel sad that in our world abortions are still necessary, and my heart aches for the women and men who must say goodbye to their unborn children.

The Diamond Sangha Ceremony on the Death of an Unborn Child

Robert Aitken, Zen teacher of the Diamond Sangha, has established *The Diamond Sangha Ceremony on the Death of an Unborn Child*, based upon the Japanese Buddhist funeral service for the *mizuko* ("water baby," the poetical term for fetus).

Aitken Roshi states, "Like any other human being that passes into the One, it is given a posthumous Buddhist name, and is thus identified as an individual, however incomplete, to whom we can say farewell. With this ceremony, the woman is in touch with life and death as they pass through her existence, and she finds that such basic changes are relative waves on the great ocean of true nature, which is not born and does not pass away.[1]

Below is the text and instructions for conducting the ceremony as adapted by Aitken Roshi and used in the Diamond Sangha and its affiliates. It may be a public or private ceremony, and may also be used in the case of miscarriage.

1. Three full bows.
2. Vandana and Ti Sarana in Pali, or Taking Refuge in English.
3. Enmei Jikku Kannon Gyo, or other short sutra in Japanese or English.
4. Leader:

   We gather today to express our love and suport for (names of parents), and to say farewell to a child unborn, a bit of being we have named (name of child), who appeared just as we all do, from the undifferentiated mind, as that mind, and who passed away after a few moments of flickering life, just as we all do.

In our culture, we place great emphasis upon maintaining life, but truly death is not a fundamental matter, but an incident, another wave. Bassui Zenji speaks of it as clouds fading in the sky. Mind essence, Bassui says, is not subject to birth or death. It is neither being nor nothingness, neither emptiness nor form and color.

It is, as Yamada Koun Roshi has said, infinite emptiness, full of possibilities, at once altogether at rest and also charged with countless tendencies awaiting the fullness of karma. Here (name of child) is in complete repose, at one with the mystery that is our own birth and death, our own no-birth and no-death.

5. Heart Sutra in Japanese or English, as parents, leader, and friends offer incense.
6. Leader:

Buddha nature pervades the whole universe,
existing right here now;
with our reciting of Enmei Jikku Kannon Gyo
let us unite with
the Ancient Seven Buddhas,
Fully Realized Shakyamuni Buddha,
Great Compassion Avalokiteshvara Bodhisattva,
Earth Treasury Ksitigarbha Bodhisattva,
all Founding Teachers, past, present, future.

We especially dedicate our love and out prayerful
thoughts to you (name of child).
May you rest in peace.

Let true Dharma continue—
Sangha relations become complete.

All:

All Buddhas throughout space and time,
all Bodhisattvas, Mahasattvas,
the Great Prajnaparamita.

7. Great Vows for All in English.
8. Three full bows.[2]

[1]Robert Aitken, *The Mind of Clover Essays in Zen Buddhist Ethics* (San Francisco: North Point, 1984), p. 22.

[2]Ibid., pp. 175-176.

At a Buddhist Temple in April

Susan Suntree

The priest is praying for you
Little Worm
Prayer for all creatures
born and unborn
Praying for parasites, curled
foetuses like ring worms, sucking
tissue of myriad women.
Little One Inch, I could still choose
not to bulge with a larger house
So I pray with the priest
being Buddhist today for your sake:
Swelling bubble of cells, afloat in the mind of love
Stretch my heart, my will, my compassion.

The Awakening of All
by Joanna Macy

In 1979, with the help of a grant from the Ford Foundation, I went to Sri Lanka to live and work for a year studying the Sarvodaya Shramadana Movement. Begun twenty years ago by a handful of high school students, Sarvodaya has become a force for change in over 5,000 villages, affecting the lives of millions of people. I wanted to study how their religious beliefs and practices shape the work of Sarvodaya workers and villagers, the majority of whom are Buddhist.

I went to live and work with them, to see how the teachings of the Buddha had been reclaimed and reinterpreted. But I wasn't just interested in making an academic study on how the use of indigenous belief systems can increase popular participation in Third World development. I was going—as a Westerner and as a Buddhist—to learn how the ancient teachings we revere can transform both individuals and societies today.

The word "Sarvodaya" means the "awakening of all." Sarvodaya is a term Gandhi invented from the Sanskrit to translate a concept that he found in Christian writers (particularly in John Ruskin's book, *Unto this Last*) based on the teaching of Jesus on compassionate action ("inasmuch as ye have done unto the last of these my brethren, ye have done it unto me"). Gandhi translated this as Sarvodaya, and defined it to mean the "uplift or welfare of all." Then, in 1958, a science teacher in a Buddhist high school in Colombo, by the name of A.T. Ariyaratne, took a handful of students on a holiday work camp. They launched a movement that consciously borrowed on Gandhian principles, while at the same time recasting these principles in Buddhist terms.

Ariyaratne took the word Sarvodaya and retranslated it, not as the uplift of all, but the awakening of all. This is what the Buddha did under the Bodhi tree. He woke up. Sarvodayans in Sri Lanka today will say "That is what development is—it is everybody waking up." It is people waking up to the conditions of their society—their own pain, the dukkha (suffering) right here, as well as to the power they have when they work together, talk together, meet and share together, and experience dana, or generosity.

In motivating people, Sarvodayans have taken Buddhist concepts and redefined them. Or, I suspect, they have restored to these practices and concepts their original meanings. For example, dana, which is generosity, the prime virtue, had come over the patriarchal centuries to mean alms-giving to the monks. Dana has now been reclaimed to mean the gift of one's time, energy, skills and knowledge to the community, as well as retaining its original meaning.

The collective sharing of energy is called shramadana (literally energy-giving) and refers specifically to a kind of work camp. The camps that were started in 1958 by Ariyaratne and his students were inspired by Quaker work camps held in Europe after World War II, adapted to a Buddhist mode. Now we in the West are learning about shramadana, and the practice flows back once again, enriched. Shramadana events here have included a "weed-out" in a Berkeley public park and an inner-city shramadana in Hartford. Sarvodaya's Buddhist inspired methods expand and deepen the event.

The work project itself is just a center linchpin. The process works like this. As a Sarvodaya organizer I am invited to come to the village. At the beginning of every Sarvodaya meeting we meditate together. Everybody comes—the men, women, children. Already that changes the chemistry, especially as the meetings begin to include song and dance, for as a Sarvodaya organizer I remind everyone that our cultural roots are a part of our wealth and power.

I explain what has been happening in shramadana in other places. And then we decide what we will accomplish in this work camp: Are we going to dig latrines or open up an access road? Clean up the irrigation canal or put a roof on the preschool? As we talk back and forth, something important happens. We are having a town meeting, or, as the movement calls it, a paule hamua, a "family gathering." The village is talking as a family. And Sarvodaya asks that people use kinship terms, which change the syntax of relationships and erase caste differences. This is called priyavachana, which in Buddhist scriptures means "pleasant speech."

Then the village plans a day when we will all work together. This day is an island in time, when we share everything—food, labor, tools.

We are not asking ourselves or each other to change for good, but just for this day of shramadana. Afterwards we can go back to life as usual. But life as usual is not the same after that, because we have had the powerful experience of sharing and working together. And we have spoken together too, because after sweating together as we heave up rocks from the path or weave palm fronds for roofing, we feel freer to say what we think and hope, even though we're a landless laborer or a school drop-out.

When I returned to this country two and a half years ago, I began adapting Sarvodayan and Buddhist ideas to a process that has come to be known as "despair and empowerment" work. These practices, inspired by Sarvodayan brothers and sisters, are very applicable here, but do not need to be identified as Buddhist. They are applicable by simply having the courage to meet people on the level of their concern, helping them break through their denial and numbness, with the recognition that there is widespread pain in our time. There is much dukkha, suffering. In our society there is a feeling of dread beyond the naming—fear and grief about the preparations for nuclear war, about the destruction of our environment, about world hunger and human oppression. After working face-to-face with many thousands of people I am convinced that this despair—or pain for the world—is felt at some level by everyone.

Up until now every generation throughout recorded history has lived with the assumption that other generations would follow. There was a tacit certainty that our children's children and those coming after would be there to carry on the work of our hands and hearts. That certainty is gone now. It is lost to us whether we work in the peace movement or the Pentagon. That loss is the central psychological reality of our time, and the suffering it induces is all the greater because people hide it. It is not considered polite or patriotic to talk about it.

But in despair and empowerment work, as it is now being carried out through the Interhelp network, it is acknowledged. And as people are helped to acknowledge and move through it, they open up to the teachings of metta (loving kindness), karuna (compassion), mudita (joy in the joy of others) and upekkha (equanimity or the great peace).

When I was coming home in 1980, I stopped in India and saw the Tibetans who had first opened the Dharma to me back in the sixties when I was living with my family in the Peace Corps in India. There, among the Tibetans in Kangra Valley, I heard references to prophecies about the coming of the kingdom of Shambhala. They stem from the Kalachakra-tantra. I was very interested in these prophecies because of their apocalyptic nature. Choegyal Rinpoche shared this interpretation of them with me.

According to the prophecies, there comes a time—and the predicted signs indicate it is the time in which we are now living—when the power of the laloes grows so great as to threaten the future of all life on earth. Laloes means barbarians. The barbarians have two centers of power: one is in the West and the other is in the center of the Eurasian land mass. Although they are sworn enemies, these two laloe powers are not very different. Both have devised, developed and continue to amass weapons of unfathomable horror and devastation. These weapons can cost us the world.

"It is in this time that the Kingdom of Shambhala appears," said Choegyal Rinpoche. It is not a geo-political entity. Rather it exists in the hearts and minds of the Shambhala warriors. A Shambhala warrior wears no uniform or insignia, wields no banner, offers no secret handshake. There are no barricades to climb upon and pontificate, or behind which they can rest or regroup. There are no boundary lines, no home turf. Ever and always they move on and through the terrain of the laloes themselves.

There comes a time when the caring and courage of these warriors becomes evident on the overt level, as they take action to dismantle the terrible weapons. In this time they go right into the very heart of the power of the barbarians—into the citadels and pit where the weapons are kept, into the corridors of power to dismantle the instruments and modalities of death. They know they can dismantle these weapons, because these weapons are manomaya—mind-made. Because they are made by the human mind they can be unmade by the human mind.

Right now the Shambhala warriors are in a period of training. "How do they train?" I asked.

"They train in the use of two weapons," Choegyal Rinpoche said. One is insight into the interdependent co-arising nature of reality. In the web of co-arising we are all so deeply interconnected that there is no "them" and no "us;" we are all one in the flow of phenomena. The other weapon is compassion, the deep energy that arises as we open to each other's suffering. Neither weapon alone is sufficient. One by itself can be cold and abstract; the other can polarize and burn us out. But with both together we can save our world.

We each have our ways of working to heal our world. In the *Perfection of Wisdom*, the *Astasahasrika Prajnaparamita*, the bodhisattva is described as flying into great space. The name of that space is the name of the mother of all Buddhas. We are invited to move into that space, to fly into it. It's the space we enter when we sit on our zafus or when we take time to connect with that space in another being. We can enter it when we are protesting nuclear weapons research at Livermore Laboratories, giving up a job in a defense industry, writing that umpteenth letter on behalf of a political prisoner for Amnesty International, joining a boycott for migrant farmers, or sitting in at a Congressional office for sane policies in Central America. We enter it as we slowly, quietly change our patterns of consumption so that our society can shift toward a sustainable culture. That space is waiting for us and we can fly into it. It liberates us from our socially-defined roles. We can fly into that space because it is the space of profound interconnectedness, where the walls between self and other fall away.

There is currently a debate in the peace movement as to whether we should treat the nuclear arms race as a single issue. We who know the dharma of interdependence know that the nuclear bomb is not separate from what is causing hunger camps, our own prisons, and the destruction of our natural life support system. We know we cannot separate out any one thing. Yet we can begin with one single issue. Seeing one thing, we can open up to see the manifold connections with all other things, all other issues.

Buddhaghosa said, "The Dharma is like a vine. You pick it up at any point and all the rest follows."

So it is with the grief of our planet-time. You can pick it up anywhere. If people want to act on the arms race, they can pick up the arms race and all else follows. And the beauty of the dharma, which you don't even need to put into Buddhist terms, is that as people own in humility their own capacity to feel the pain of our time—they can, by the same measure—own their inter-relatedness. It stems from a deep source. Call it the mind of God. Call it Buddha-nature. We all want to come home to it.

Practicing Intimacy

Fran Tribe

In ancient times, if you wanted to practice Zen, you had to go to a monastery or training temple. You would sit zazen, chant, study sutras or koans, go to dokusan, and do a lot of bowing and offering of incense. These are basic forms of Zen practice. The work of maintaining the monastery, cooking, going to town to ask for alms, etc., is also considered part of training in most places. These are recognized forms of meditation in action. But although there have always been serious lay practitioners, until now marriage and household life have remained outside the realm of what was widely considered "Zen practice." Historically, the monk's path and the householder's path were parallel. Now they converge considerably. There are many stories about enlightened laypeople, but we don't know how they manifested their understanding in their domestic relationships or how they managed to balance the demands of family life with those of religious training or formal practice.

In the last chapter of *Zen Mind Beginner's Mind*, Suzuki Roshi says, "American students are not priests and yet not completely laymen... that you are not priests is an easy matter, but that you are not exactly laymen is more difficult... You are on your way to discovering some appropriate form of life."

When Suzuki Roshi gave that talk, he had ordained only a few American priests, but he had a pretty clear idea from his own experience of what a priest's life was like. Most of us were young and hadn't started families yet. We were former flower children; it was, I think, 1969. A lot has changed since then, and the question of what is an appropriate way to live and practice as "not quite priests and not completely laymen" is more complex for most of us now that we are older. For instance, many of the priests, in our community and others, are married and have children. Being ordained no longer means leaving household life. Most of the Zen students I know are involved in some kind of intimate relationship and are trying to find ways to take care of their relationships, careers and households as part of "practice." Because our expectations of an intimate relationship and family life are quite different from those of previous generations (and radically different from what was the norm in Japan when Suzuki Roshi married), we are very much on our own as we experiment with appropriate forms of practice and lifestyle.

Many students are frustrated by the lack of guidance they find in the literature and the scarcity of role models past or present. But priest or layperson, those of us who find ourselves equally committed to both marriage and Zen training find we have no choice but to use everything in our life as a form of "practice." Because our everyday lives are so busy, we don't have a lot of time for bowing, chanting and zazen. But our days are filled with the many naturally occurring practice forms such as washing dishes, making love and going to work.

Formal practice helps us still the mind and see into our true nature. We should make good use of the traditional forms. But we should also remember that the naturally occurring forms have the same teaching value. Whether we're in the zendo or home in bed, "form is not different from emptiness, emptiness is not different from form," as the Heart Sutra says. What we call "Zen practice" is not different from raising our children or learning how to get along with our partners. The koan of relationship is: how can I be true to myself and be in harmony with another? This is everyone's koan. It contains the essential questions common to many standard koans: What is self? What is other? What is this? Married or single, male or female, priest or layperson, these questions are central to us all, on the cushion, in dokusan, and at home.

Discovering a spiritual practice is a lot like falling in love. We're attracted to something for various reasons, some of them idealistic, others connected with desire. We may be attracted to Zen or some other practice because we are looking for a way out of the suffering we feel. We may choose something which appeals to our aesthetic sense or something which is intellectually stimulating. Perhaps we are impressed with a teacher who seems to embody many of the qualities we consider ideal.

Our idealism gives us the energy to overcome many of the difficulties and rigors of beginning to practice. And confidence that we have chosen the "best" practice or the "true" teacher often gives us the courage to drop old habits and try something new. A good teacher, it is said, arouses the thought of enlightenment and encourages us to realize our own enlightened nature.

We choose a partner for similarly mixed reasons, many of them unconscious. Sexual attractiveness may play a big role in our choice and sometimes overshadows what we later perceive to be flaws in our partner's personality. People also tend to choose mates whose strengths complement their own weaknesses. We all know lots of couples where one person is a thinker whose feeling side is weak and the other is a feeling person whose thinking side is weak. Very often the partner we choose manifests some quality which is trying to come out in us. More often than not, however, rather than developing our weak side by learning from the other, we passively allow our partner to complete us, and each of us becomes increasingly one-sided. This happens with teachers and students, too.

Few of us are untouched by the myth that there is a "perfect" partner for everyone, a prince charming for every princess. This same kind of mythology guides our search for the right practice, teacher or center. It's very hard to give up looking outside our own self for "the answer."

In both spiritual practice and marriage, the first phase consists of merging with our ideal. In Zen, merger is both cultivated and expressed through zazen. Sometimes we call it samadhi. In an intimate relationship we cultivate and express our oneness in sexual union. In any event, merging is a fusion of body, mind, and this moment. But samadhi, like all states of mind, is not permanent; and even the greatest lovers cannot stay in bed all the time. Oneness and separateness, enlightenment and delusion, exist together; you can't have one without the other. Our subjective state of mind is constantly changing along with everything else. There is simply no comfortable resting place. This is a great disappointment!

In both practice and marriage, the honeymoon phase gives way to the next phase and we begin to notice the faults of our partner, the weaknesses of our teacher, the things we don't like about the tradition or practice situation we've gotten ourselves into. Merger gives way to separateness. We long for that golden state of oneness, but our desire to merge with perfection remains unsatisfied because we know we've chosen something imperfect. A lot of people give up at this point. Many others stay in the situation and blame their unhappiness or the lack of inner peace on the faults of their partner or teacher. We all tend to get caught by the illusion that a situation is either good or it's bad. It's terribly hard to contain both sides.

The truth is that every situation is both flawed and perfect. Our teacher knows something but not everything. We can get the Dharma from him or her in spite of his or her flaws, but often we'd rather use these flaws as an excuse for not making that strenuous effort. It's possible to let go of idealism without falling into disillusionment. It's possible, but for most of us, it's very difficult.

Many of us fall in and out of love repeatedly and/or go from one practice, teacher or healer to another endlessly in search of perfection, satisfaction, and peace of mind. We go from being totally merged with something to being totally isolated. This life is like a rollercoaster lurching from bliss to despair and back again. We all have some tendency to be this way, but we all have the opportunity to live our lives in a balanced way that is not so shaken by the ups and downs which are bound to come along. How do we balance our lives as "not quite priests and not completely laypeople?"

It can start with a vow. Vows express our inner decision to live in a certain way in spite of impulses which might lead us in another direction. Marriage vows express publicly a couple's private commitment to their relationship. The vows or "I will's" of marriage go with "I won't's," the self-limits to which we agree. These are the ten prohibitory precepts. When we agree to give up the "freedom" of single life, we may not realize that we've actually agreed to give up our preoccupation with our separate self. The ceremonies we use for marriage, for priest ordination, and for *jukai* (sometimes called lay ordination) are almost identical. The core of our basic ceremony is the Bodhisattva precepts, because our commitment is to live for the benefit of others, letting go of personal preference and making the effort to act in the common interest.

Popular mythology notwithstanding, marriage is not an avenue for satisfying all of our desires; and Zen practice isn't a way to get rid of them once and for all. Both are tools for recognizing desire as it arises and taming that energy for more conscious use. In the version of the Four Vows we chant here in Berkeley we say, "Desires are inexhaustible, I vow to put an end to them." This sounds so absolute and so hard that we're liable to give up, rather like the dieter who, after a disappointing encounter with the scale, heads for the refrigerator.

Desire isn't bad. It's just our life energy expressing itself. One aspect of desire that gets us in trouble is wanting something we don't have or wanting things to be some way they aren't. We can use this energy or be used by it. When we use our energy more consciously, we can bring what is and what we desire into closer harmony—one breath at a time, one moment at a time, paying full attention to what comes up.

Paying attention in this way to our internal states is different from indulging, judging or acting on them. Paying full attention, we are completely intimate with our situation. We're not separate from our circumstances. Suzuki Roshi used to say that when thoughts come up in zazen we shouldn't invite them to tea. Neither should we slam the door in their face. Too often when our teachers advise us to "sit with" our feelings and problems, we sit on them instead. In our eagerness to attain equanimity and look like a buddha, we may squelch "undesirable" states of mind. This is just another kind of attachment, and it's no better than getting up and storming around every time we feel angry.

We can experience feelings without thinking of doing something about them, just as we can sit still even when our legs hurt without denying the pain. The self-protective walls begin to crumble and we learn to accept what *is*.

Repressing feelings, indulging or justifying them, and expressing them inappropriately all cut off the possibility of truly letting go of them. Both types of mistakes lead to more and more suffering. In zazen and at other times, our mind is full of conflicting thoughts and impulses. We like some of them better than others. As long as we allow our life to be led by our preferences alone, we suffer and make others suffer. As long as we blame our lack of progress toward inner peace on the faults of our teachers and our domestic unhappiness solely on the problems of our partner, we continue to be stuck. Behind the Bodhisattva vow is a vow to be fully responsible for our own inner and outer life. Until we are ready to take that silent vow, nothing we say out loud about our formal practice or our everyday life means very much.

Dogen describes zazen as taking the "backward step that turns our light inward to illuminate the true self." Turning inward with the light off leads to repression. Turning the light outward, we see the faults of others without seeing our own shadow. In zazen, our immobile body expresses willingness to contain all the good, bad, or indifferent stuff that comes to us and through us. We have to open our mind until, like Vimilakirti's house, it holds everything. We'd rather contain only the good stuff, transcendent thoughts and celestial beings. But transcending duality means allowing both the feeling of the moment and its opposite to exist within us at the same time. We hold them both in the palm of our left hand.

At one moment the palm of my hand might hold something like this:

> Right now, I'm furious with my husband, in touch with my anger,
> *and* aware that I love him, *and* aware that we're not different.

> Right now, my friend has hurt me. I'm angry and hurt. I recognize my friend's suffering and confusion as my own and vow to offer the support I would like to receive.

Fundamentally, the opposites we must contain in a relationship are oneness and separateness. If unity dominates, we have a symbiotic relationship in which neither person can make it alone. If separateness dominates, there's no deep intimacy, and the connection is incomplete. In the *Sandokai*, Sekito says, "To be attached to things, this is delusion; but just to understand that all is one is not enough... Within the light there is darkness, but do not be attached to that darkness. Within the darkness there is light, but do not be caught by that light. Light and darkness are a pair, like the foot before and the foot behind in walking."

Onesness and separateness are a pair, like the foot before and the foot behind in walking. Until we have some actual experience of this, we just have to limp along as best we can, dragging the other foot. After we have some experience of it, the path continues forever, but we feel encouraged to continue our step-by-step effort.

With apologies to Sekito, "I say respectfully to those who seek the way, do not vainly pass through sunshine and shadows."

The Listening Place
A Zen Story for Children
Deborah Hopkinson

A long long time ago, there was a girl named Myo who lived with her family in Japan. Their little cottage was on the side of big mountain covered with meadows and pine trees. At the top of the mountain, there was the great temple of Bassui Zenji.

Each week, Myo went with her parents and other neighbors up to the top of the mountain to visit the temple. She liked to look at the smooth floors that shone like mirrors. She could even see herself in them. She liked to watch the long rows of monks chanting all together.

But most of all she liked the sounds of the bells. There were all kinds of temple bells. Some bells helped the monks to keep time while they chanted. Some bells announced that Bassui Zenji had arrived to give a talk. But the biggest and most beautiful bell of all was the great temple bell, which rang early every morning calling all the people to come to the temple. That bell woke up the whole mountain!

After the monks chanted, Bassui Zenji would stand up and talk to all the parents and children, too. Myo like Bassui Zenji. He was skinny and had a very bald head. His head was shiny just like the floors in the temple. And he always smiled at her and said hello as if he really was glad to see her. Sometimes Myo didn't listen very carefully because she was thinking about a story she had read, or about a tree in the meadow she wanted to climb, or a bird's nest she wanted to visit. And sometimes she listened very carefully but she could not understand all that the old man said because she was so little.

But one day, Bassui Zenji started to talk about birds. Myo liked birds more than just about anything, and so she lifted up her head and listened very very carefully.

Bassui Zenji was talking about how to listen to the birds sing. That's funny, thought Myo, everyone can listen to birds sing!

"You do not really hear the birds," said Bassui Zenji. "You must ask yourself the question, 'Who hears?' You must go to the place of 'really listening' to the birds—and to all the other sounds—the wind in the trees, the temple bell in the morning, the woodcutter's axe in the forest."

Myo wondered about this. Where could she go to really hear the birds? Where was the listening place that Bassui Zenji was talking about?

She wanted to ask him, or to ask her mother or father, but she was too shy. Maybe I am the only one who doesn't know, she thought.

And so Myo decided that she would find the listening place all by herself. She loved to play in the fields and the pine forest near her cottage. After school, she would go and help her mother and father, and then she would be free to play and explore. She liked to look for flowers, hidden behind the stumps of old trees, and to watch the little mushrooms poke their heads out from under the moss.

Now, whenever Myo went to play, she tried to listen very hard to the birds. She listened to the birds while she sat at the top of a pine tree, where she could feel herself swaying gently every time the breeze blew.

She listened while she lay leaning against a warm rock on the hill, or when she was lying on the soft grass in the field looking up at the clouds rolling by.

Myo heard all kinds of birds. She heard the songs of the thrushes, the loud call of the bush warbler, and the soft voices of doves.

But still, she could not find the listening place that Bassui had talked about.

"Maybe it is at the temple," she thought. So one day she walked by herself to the top of the hill and sat in the temple garden.

It was a beautiful garden. It had a little stream and a bridge, and there was even a stone bench to sit on. Myo sat for awhile listening very hard.

Then she noticed that the old teacher, Bassui Zenji, had come to sit beside her. He smiled.

"Hello, Myo. You are sitting here very quietly," he said.

"Yes," said Myo. "I am looking for the listening place that you told us about. I want to really hear the birds."

"Oh," he said, "Where have you been looking?"

"Well, I looked in the forest, and in the field, and in the top of a pine tree," said Myo.

"Those are good places to listen," said Bassui Zenji. "This is a good place, too. And whenever you come here, I will help you find the listening place. Do you hear the sparrow now?"

Myo sat on the bench with the old teacher for a little while. There were a lot of birds. She listened very hard. First there was a sparrow...chirp chirp chirp...and then everything was very quiet. And then a little thrush starting calling to its mother to feed it—chirrup chirrup chirrup. After it flew away, Myo could hear a bush warbler crying out high in the trees—toowee, toowee, toowee.

One by one the birds sang and then it was quiet again. It felt good to sit and listen. She listened so hard she even forgot that she was trying to find the listening place.

"What do you hear?" asked the old teacher.

Just then a big crow called overhead.

"Caw, caw," said Myo. Then she laughed. Bassui Zenji laughed too.

All of a sudden the gong sounded for supper.

"It is time for all of us to eat," said Bassui Zenji. "Come back and sit with me in our listening place sometime soon."

"And remember, the listening place is always just where you are."

Myo laughed and ran all the way home, listening to the birds in the trees and to the sounds that her feet made in the pine needles.

"I can really listen all the time!" she said to herself. And she did.

Author's Note: This story is based on the famous Koan used by the Japanese Zen Master Bassui: "Who is the master of that sound?"

This story was written for a young friend, Keelia Hemphill Johnston. I would also like to dedicate it to the memory of my mother, Gloria D. Hopkinson.

Voices of Women Teachers

Attention

Flora Courtois

At the heart of our Zen practice there is a kind of radically intimate attention. This absolutely firsthand quality of experience characterizes the beginning of our lives and, if we are not drugged, the end. No "other" mediates between us and the intimate aloneness of birth. No memories, no thoughts, no plans invade this pure innerness with their shadowing images. So, too, is the spare simplicity of our deaths.

Here attention is reality and reality attention.

But in the days and years of our living somehow we lose touch with this clarity and think to possess ourselves in images. In so doing, we fall into a bad case of mistaken identity. We think our living instead of living our thinking. In the language of koan study, we miss the point of life and so live at second, third and fourth hand.

Yet the opportunity to be restored to our original, unborn, divine condition is always immediately at hand. There are no real or absolute contingencies.

Every moment lived in absorbed attention is simultaneously a beginning and an end, at once a birth and a death. In such attention we are radically open to the unexpected, to letting life live us. Any event, however small or seemingly trivial, properly attended, opens the door to infinity.

In Basho's famous haiku, the plopping sound of the frog jumping into the clear still pond rises whole, perfect and infinitely mysterious. No time here for meaning to be added or we'll miss the next plop as it comes.

There's a bit of Faust in us all, believing as we do that the more we learn about something the closer we are to it. Not so. Any event, fully attended, uproots all our knowing at the source and carries inexhaustible surprises.

To use the language of instrument design, we may say that when we quiet all the interfering noises in our system we then maximize the information in the messages we pick up and transmit.

Yasutani Roshi said that shikantaza (just sitting) is like standing in a clearing in a deep forest, knowing danger is about to strike but not knowing from what direction. If we focus too much ahead we will miss it if it comes from below and so on. Total, uncluttered readiness for the unexpected is what we need. If we think we've got it at one moment we may lose it the next.

A few years ago, a young couple moved into an apartment across from the Zen Center of Los Angeles. The girl, Mary, had been in a mental hospital and several people were concerned because they thought she was troubled once again. They had urged her to try Yoga and Zen and other ways to no avail and so I was asked to talk to her. Making no promises, I went across the street to find Mary all crumpled up like a bird with a broken wing, sitting at the end of a sofa in a dark apartment. Sitting down and taking her hand, I said, "Mary, do you want to tell me where you are right now?"

She then told me about a bad nightmare she had had which she couldn't forget, where she seemed to be going down a long passageway, dark and frightening, to a room where somebody pulled her in and closed the door and where she found herself with several threatening figures and no way out.

"All right," I said, "Now, would you like to know where I am right now?"

She said, "Yes."

I said, "Well, we're just going to listen to any sound that comes along, absolutely nothing else." So we sat for quite a while, holding hands, listening very quietly.

Then I said, "Now do you hear a car go by... a bird chirp... a little boy crying... a plane overhead? Do you see if we keep remembering the car we won't hear the bird? If we try to plan what's coming next, we won't hear it. If we even use the words 'listening' or think 'I am listening' we will miss it. Nothing is ever repeated or predictable or the same but all is unexpectedly fresh if we listen this way. This is listening the way a cat listens, a kind of listening with the back of your mind, just letting be without any hesitation or interference. You can do that, can't you?"

Mary said, "Yes."

I said, "Then as long as you know you can you're home safe, right where you've always been and always will be. You really don't have to practice Yoga or Zen or anything else right now. So let's go to dinner, shall we?"

Mary put on her coat and we went out to a nearby restaurant where she talked very insightfully about her experiences in the mental hospital: how the doctors need sick people so they can be doctors and how the sick people need a hospital and doctors so they can be sick people.

I hear from Mary every once in a while or I hear about her. I heard about her just a week ago. She's getting along very well. She has a job, no more problems; I mean no more serious ones.

Obviously, just remembering how to listen is not all there is to zazen. The point is that all phenomena, all dharmas, whether seen or heard or felt or whatever and whether pleasurable or painful, it matters not, all without exception, open us to reality if we give ourselves to them. "How can we know the dancer from the dance?" wrote William Butler Yeats. Zen says the whole universe is art and we are the artists.

"God," wrote Meister Eckhart, "has left a little point where the soul turns back upon itself and finds itself." At another time he described God's little point this way, "The eye by which I see God is the same eye by which God sees me. My eye and God's eye are one and the same."

"To have satori," wrote D. T. Suzuki, "is to stand at Meister Eckhart's little point, where we may see in two directions at once, God's way and creature's way."

"Attention, attention, attention," wrote Zen Master Ikkyu many centuries ago when asked to write down the highest wisdom.

"But what does attention mean?" asked his questioner.

Master Ikkyu replied, "Attention means attention."

Surely Meister Eckhart's eye, which is simultaneously God's eye, is the inner eye of imminent, transcendent attention. Quieting the busy surface of our minds, we free our inner eye to find that little point which penetrates right to the inner heart of things. No need to look for vast, cosmic fireworks or for a great big impressive way to enlightenment if we enlighten each moment with attention.

True attention is rare and totally sacrificial. It demands that we throw away everything we have been or hope to be, to face each moment naked of identity, open to whatever comes and bereft of human guidance.

Nor is the potential for pain to be underestimated. Now we come face to face with the radical fact that there is nothing, however dear, that cannot be taken from us from one moment to the next; nothing, however sinister or horrifying, from which we will be permitted to recoil or separate ourselves. All the dreadful, mute suffering from which inattention shielded us will now be seen and heard.

Another name for such full attention is love.

In Christian terms, surely in God's presence the appropriate behavior is to be quiet and listen. The essence of prayer is attention. To pray is to go directly to God, without intermediary, and to say *nothing*.

There's been a great deal said in the last ten years about personal growth and about exploring one's "inner" self. Participants at countless conferences have been encouraged to get in touch with blocked feelings, tensions, untapped potential, dreams, etc. Other conferences are held on the "whole person," "holistic medicine," in which psychology plus ESP plus body awareness and so on, are all added together, as if to put Humpty Dumpty together again.

There's no contradiction with Zen practice in all this, provided we realize that the phenomena of the so-called "inner" person: emotions, feelings and so on, are just as much phenomena or dharmas as the "external" ones of chasing money or building businesses. They are all equally phenomena and all "outer" in the sense that Zen practice is inner to them all.

Nor do we necessarily become whole by attending conferences, however useful, where we learn to know more and more about this and that.

To be absorbed in emptiness is not to know at all. In the radical *unknowing* of pure attention we sacrifice ourselves and discover our original wholeness.

Although we sacrifice our very lives for the good of all humankind, if self-images distract our attention we become separated from the true reality of our living and dying. For the ultimate revolutionary act is not giving up our lives literally but direct, immediate seeing which is our own true nature. Such radical seeing is the heart of Buddhism and Zen practice.

So let us keep our "beginner's mind." Only so will we continually discover "the dearest freshness deep-down things."

For A More Harmonious Life

Charlotte Joko Beck

We're all here either because we're doing Zen practice or because we're interested in it. The question of course is "What is it? What are we doing? And why is it a practice at all?"

In a certain sense this wonderful life that we're right in the middle of—which is ourself—is complete and perfect from the very beginning. And all we have to do is just realize that. Most of you have heard this many times before, and yet we continue to sit and struggle. Why?

The reason is that we determine personally to be the center of all this... and we're not. We are it, but we're not the center. So, one way of looking at our practice is to make this multiplicity of little selves that we entertain into a unity. Christ said, "He who loseth his life shall find it." And Dogen Zenji said the same thing, "To study the self is to forget the self. And to forget the self is to be enlightened by all things." Go from a multiplicity to a unity.

Some years ago, in my koan study with Maezumi Roshi, he said to me that there are two parts in presenting a koan. The first part is the presentation: how do you present the spirit of the koan? The second part is to realize the truth of this koan in your life itself. And as many of you know, most people studying koans are doing something with the first part and quite often forgetting about the second part. Roshi said to me at that time, "I want you from now on to shift your life from 'why' to 'how'." That's all he said, and it took me a while to figure out what he meant.

Shift your life from "why" to "how." "Why" is the multiplicity of little questions we have centered around this little self, even the wonderful questions such as, "Why are we here?" The kind of question which runs our life more than any other is: "Why is my life this way?" "Why is this happening to me?" In other words, "Why isn't it the way I want it?" When life is coming in at you, not in a pleasant way, you say "Why?"

Shifting to "how" is simply asking the question, "How can I make this life, right now, more harmonious?" "What can I do, not in some big grand sense, but right now, in this present problem I'm stuck in?" Not, "Why is this happening to me?" but, "How can I create more harmony?" That's what Roshi was asking of me. There are many ways of looking at this practice, and one is to make this shift from "why" to "how."

"Why" is the personal confusion we all have. Each one of us is like a pie, split into all sorts of little selves. Each slice wants something different. There's our greed, our anger, our need to be important—or to be unimportant, our resentment, our wanting this or that—wanting to be enlightened even, our wanting success of whatever sort—or our not being able to face having success. All these are for each one of us a little pie that we're split into. It'll look a little different with each person, but basically we're all split into wanting something and then wondering why we don't have it. At different times, depending on the stimulus, we're caught in one piece of that pie or another. And occasionally different pieces of the pie even fight with each other.

The first stage of any life, to some degree, is being caught in some piece of that pie. Then somewhere along the line, depending on what happens in our life, we become aware that we're caught... if we're smart. If we're not smart, we just suffer and it doesn't do us any good at all.

The third stage is much more interesting: it's when we begin to see that the only way out of this being caught is to directly experience the place where we're stuck. If it's anger, to experience the anger; resentment, to experience the resentment. This experience is always bodily; it has nothing to do with getting lost in the thoughts in your mind! It's when this problem that we're caught in, seemingly from external factors, begins to settle into the body, that the transformation begins. It's not the thoughts! It's the settling into that direct bodily experience. It's a process of awareness.

Sooner or later, working like this, we become really aware that my pie and your pie aren't much different. And out of this insight there begins to be some compassion for ourselves and for other people. We can have the angriest set of feelings about somebody, but as we become more aware of the total process, this compassion appears and grows. But the compassion never comes if we're not being aware of what's really going on with us.

There's a stage after this awareness and compassion that starts the cycle into stronger and stronger practice. It's when we really see what mischief we're up to in being stuck with our particular drives and desires. It's not that there may be anything wrong with those desires in themselves, but being caught by them, we do mischief. So this next stage of practice is repentance.

Repentance doesn't mean guilt. It means just really seeing what we've done out of our separateness; and then begins the process of being at-one-ment.

The cycle goes on, and on, and on. And as it goes on, our will to do it increases. As we become aware of what mischief we're up to, our desire to repent appears; and the desire to practice comes out of that. This is the strengthening of what I'd call will. Will is the unity of purpose that emerges when you experience yourself honestly without excluding anything.

Will is a rather unpopular term in modern times. It has a connotation of a horse trainer training a horse. That is, I'm making some part of me do something else. That's the usual understanding of will power. But it's not what I'm talking about at all. Will in Zen practice is that central resolve which comes out of this multiplicity of ourselves becoming unity. And as we practice, the will just gets stronger and stronger.

Many of you may know of Shibayama Roshi, mainly through his books, *Zen Comments on the Mumonkan* and *A Flower Does Not Talk*. Shibayama Roshi was a very fine teacher in the Rinzai lineage. One of the things he said on this subject was:

> It is not easy for anyone to cast away the chain of ignorance and discrimination all at once. A very strong will is required. And one has to search single-heartedly for one's true self within oneself. Hard training is needed in Zen. And it never resorts to an easy-going, instant means.

Most basically, will comes out of the willingness to face fear and pain. At the bottom of all our little numbers, all these little pieces of our pie, there's fear. We do everything in life rather than face that fear. I've talked about it before; our skill in this evasion is infinite. We may not be so good at some other things, but we're really good at that. We can cover up that fear endlessly. When we're willing to face all the pieces of our pie: our drives, our cruelty, everything that we have inside of us; out of that comes the will, the compassion, and the freedom.

There's a story about the Buddha. The man next to him is asleep, having a dream. He's thrashing around, obviously frightened. He keeps saying, "There's a tiger after me." He's suffering greatly in his dream.

Obviously there's nothing he can do except to wake up from that dream. The Buddha is watching him; there's no way he can do anything about that tiger. The man in the dream has to turn around, face what he's afraid of, and wake up. Then the tiger will disappear and so will his fear and suffering. He'll see it was only a dream.

If we face our fear directly, we find a paper tiger that has no depth; it's empty. And facing it—the phoenix rises from the ashes, the flowers bloom on the withered tree.

That's the process. And for a student of Zen, the problem is: over the years how do we continue to develop our will? This is what Zen training essentially is.

There are a couple of aspects of will. Will can be very soft, very skillful, very yielding. It doesn't have to be rigid and forceful. When the will is completely developed we can hold all the parts of ourselves, without suppressing anything. And we can use it in whatever way we want. That's real strength.

Another aspect of will is intention. It's absolutely basic to our practice. A lot of people flop down on their cushions and then count their breaths sort of mechanically—shallowly—without really paying attention to the process, putting themselves into it very little. That's not good practice. There has to be, behind every breath, your intention. It doesn't matter what your practice is. There are many techniques in Zen training, but the most important thing, like the rug under your feet, is the foundation, your intention—the intention to wake up, the intention to train.

Actually, until a person has some glimmer, something that arouses that intention, there's nothing anyone can do. A person can be suffering greatly in life, but until something gets through, some insight, "I need to do something," the best teacher in the world is helpless. There has to be that little bit of awakening. Then the process is to take that little piece and enlarge it with the cycle that we've been talking about.

Over the years, our will, our clarity, our compassion, will just naturally grow. Then we'll move from this "why" to "how," from multiplicity to unity. The personal experience and the universal experience will merge. And our attitudes in training will become like the phrase from the Bible: "not my will but thine be done." It's not that there's some will outside of yourself, but a feeling that you and this universe are one. There's no separation in what you want for yourself, and what you want for everything else.

The way to accomplish this experience, and all the stages I mentioned, is to practice... continuously through the years. It isn't easy to maintain practice for such a long time. In a way, we don't want to do it.

We'd rather have the drama, play our own little trips. As Shibayama Roshi said, it's hard. But the benefits, for ourselves, and for everyone else, are more than worth it. So please continue, and do the practice. Thank you.

An Interview with Joan Rieck, Joun Roshi

Eileen Kiera

Joan Rieck was born and raised in Manitowoc, Wisconsin. She joined the Maryknoll Mission Sisters and was sent to Japan where she had her first introduction to Zen in the mid-sixties. In 1972, she began studying with Yamada Koun Roshi in Kamakura, and received permission to teach from him in 1983. Later that same year, Joan began studying at the Jung Institute in Zurich, Switzerland. She currently divides her time between Zen groups in Lucerne, Switzerland and Seattle, Washington. This conversation took place in Seattle in June 1985.

Q. What was the origin of your spiritual life, and how did you eventually come to study Zen?

A. My original religious inspiration probably came from my mother, who was a very devout Catholic. I had an intense spiritual life as a child. During high school I was more interested in my social life, but when I reached college, I was almost constantly occupied by the question "What is the meaning of life?" A friend and I used to sit on the floor talking about this for hours. It was a burning question for me. Finally I decided to drop out of school and join the Maryknoll Mission Sisters.

I was very happy at Maryknoll and thrilled when I was sent to Japan, where I became fascinated by the people and the culture. My first contact with Zen came in Japan in the mid-sixties, when I heard Fr. Lasalle, a German Jesuit now in his eighties, speak to a group of Christians about Zen. Shortly after the *Three Pillars of Zen* came out I read it and tried to practice on my own, sitting by myself as described in the book, but my practice was sporadic.

In the late 60's I decided to leave the convent and I went back to school to do graduate work in anthropology with a focus on Japanese religion. While I was in graduate school, I had a personal crisis and suffered a kind of deep depression. I couldn't pray, but I found I could sit quietly in zazen. At the height of my crisis, I had a transforming experience but didn't really understand it. In 1971, I had the chance to return to Japan on a research grant and once there, I spent some interesting months in the Japanese backwoods studying the traditional religious life. But when I tried to put my data together into a dissertation I kept getting sick to my stomach. I realized I wanted to practice Japanese religion, not analyze it. A Maryknoll friend introduced me to Yamada Roshi and the San-un Zendo in Kamakura and I felt I had found my way again. I never went back to the University, though I kept my research data in a box in my closet all those years. I just threw it out this spring when I went back to clear out of my apartment in Kamakura.

Q. Do you still feel like a Christian?

A. I've never felt as though I've left the Church, but certainly I've left many of my former understandings about Christianity behind. Actually I don't feel like a Christian or a Buddhist. I can't put myself into one category. Christianity has had a very big influence in my life, but so has Zen, perhaps even more than Christianity.

Q. How did you see your role as a teacher when you were a Maryknoll sister?

A. As a missioner I spent most of the time teaching English. I didn't speak the Japanese language well enough at that time to do religious teaching. But of course, I was there with the intention of introducing Christianity to the Japanese.

Q. How do you view your role as a teacher of Zen?

A. It was hard for me to decide to begin to teach. Then I realized that if I were just present, saying yes to the moment, to the requests of some people who were asking me to teach, it would take care of itself. So I simply opened myself up to that and tried to let go of any concern about what "I" could do. I always have the feeling that the less I get in the way, the better things go. I try to allow myself to be used in a place, responding to the needs of the moment.

Q. Have you had any difficulty in reconciling the theology of Catholicism with the idea of emptiness in Zen?

A. Of course when I first started to practice this question came up, but Yamada Roshi always said to put such questions on the shelf and to come back to them after one knew what the Way was. When I came to know Zen better, they ceased being a problem. In the experience called kensho there is no theology, no religion, nothing called Zen. This experience can happen to anyone, anywhere, regardless of religion. It is beyond the relative world of religion, and to call it the "Zen experience" is misleading because the Christian or Jew who goes far enough comes to the same point. In trying to express it, each person uses the language of their own world view. As ways or religions, Zen and Christianity are different traditions. On an intellectual level, they are probably irreconcilable—the concepts of the void and of a personal God, for example. Yet often mystics and Zen masters make the same kind of statements. No doubt they come out of experiences of the same Reality. Experiences that seem to point to a different reality must still be connected to some level of the relative world where differences are based on what is in the individual psyche. If they have any religious color at all, they are not the kensho experience of "not one thing."

Q. Do you think that training in Christianity leads people to that experience?

A. Yes, it can, but the path is not so clearly taught anymore. That's changing, however. Recently there has been a great surge of interest in contemplative prayer in the church.

In order to surrender or lose yourself, which is the prerequisite for realization of the True Self, it can be very helpful to have an idea of a personal God to surrender to. Here the Christian has an advantage, but when such a person has a real kensho and finds nothing at all in the void, it can be extremely difficult to accept. The True Fact does not change, of course, regardless of our ideas about it, but it is painful to give up the image of God one has worshipped. In this respect, the Zen practitioner may be better prepared for kensho. The desire for a personal God is deep-rooted. It could be, as Gerald May has pointed out, that having God as an object is the ego's way of hanging on to its delusive stance as an independent subject.

Q. Yamada Roshi spoke of Zen as being a dying religion in Japan. Do you see it being revitalized by the move to the West, and by the new ties that are being developed with Christianity?

A. I have the feeling that there's a great future for Zen in the West, or perhaps for something else developing out of Zen. It doesn't matter if Zen dies as long as people experience their True Self. Maybe an even greater way will develop. I don't know what it's going to be like in several hundred years, but I think Zen is already playing an important role in the change of consciousness that is now taking place. And I believe that Zen and Christianity can learn from each other. Zen presents a structured and systematic way of practice, and has perhaps influenced a reviving of the Christian tradition of objectless contemplation. On the other hand, I have found some Christian writers, like Brother Lawrence and St. John of the Cross, whose descriptions of the steps that a person may go through along the way are not found in such detail in Zen literature.

Q. Are you experimenting with rituals and forms that are traditionally used in Zen practice?

A. I don't see myself experimenting right now. I want to use the basic forms that have developed over the centuries: zazen, dokusan, teisho, the use of koans and the practice of breath counting, breath watching or shikantaza, sutras, and Zen verses. I imagine that with time a peculiarly Western expression of the Zen experience will develop in an organic way. In the meantime, I hope to transmit as purely as possible the essentials of the traditional way I have learned. We are primarily a lay group and I don't think we need to be as formal as they are in the monasteries of Japan, so I put less emphasis on formality in the practice. And by reducing the amount of ritual we can make it easier for non-Buddhists to practice Zen. There are other Zen groups around that can fulfill the need of persons who want to have a strong Buddhist devotional life, and I recognize that this is a felt need for some persons, especially if they have never had a devotional life in another religion. I also give extensive explanations about the rituals we do perform so people don't automatically interpret them from a Christian viewpoint which doesn't always apply in Zen. I'd like to keep those aspects of Zen that aid the practice and leave behind those that come purely from Japanese culture.

Q. I'm interested in how you see the Japanese culture forms affecting Zen and how you think those forms may change in the West.

A. I don't feel we have to take on anything that's obviously only a Japanese cultural form. Adopting Japanese customs can make Zen practice unnecessarily strange and difficult. I think we should eat Western foods off Western dishes with knife, fork and spoon. Even the Japanese don't eat cheese sandwiches from rice bowls. They use plates for that. I feel the same about dress and language. I have some questions about the sound of chanting in English, for example. With the Sino-Japanese, the "bup, bup, bup," of the mokugyo fits very well because of the nature of the language. But when I hear English done that way, it sounds to me like a violation of English. So for right now, we're just reciting the sutras and Zen verses in English. When I hear the Four Vows chanted here in Japanese I also feel uncomfortable because they are not pronounced properly. Both the Japanese and the English chanting done in our group sound very unnatural to me. I think this is one of the problems we need to work on. As yet, I'm not sure of the solution, but it's something I hope we can work out satisfactorily in the future. For the time being, we're just reciting in English. I would like to do chanting in English if we can find an appropriate way to do it.

Q. Some teachers in the United States have done away with much of Buddhist ritual and replaced it with a psychological perspective. I know you have studied Jungian psychology, as well as Zen. How do you view psychology as it relates to Zen?

A. It can give us a psychological interpretation of what is happening in our practice, but not a "spiritual" interpretation. I think it's helpful for a spiritual teacher to have some background in psychology, but I don't believe he or she needs to be a therapist or should be expected to do therapy. Psychology is not Zen. Although it can be helpful to a student if a teacher talks about some aspects of the Way from a psychological viewpoint, the world of Zen transcends psychological interpretation, and has its own language. Zen deals with a level of our being which psychological constructs cannot reach. And it leads to an inexplicable experience that we can only attempt to describe by speaking in paradoxes and parables. Psychology can comment on the psychological aspects of practicing Zen but only from its own limited level of knowing.

Q. Jung spoke a lot about the collective unconscious. Does this concept approach the Zen experience of oneness from a psychological viewpoint?

A. No, I don't think so. As I understand it, the unconscious is a name for everything we are not consciously aware of. Empty-oneness, which is the heart of the Zen experience, is the essence of the universe, conscious and unconscious. But people can only experience oneness with what they are conscious of.

Q. Do you think psychological understanding is an aid in Zen practice?

A. From my short teaching experience, I feel that being in therapy, or having completed therapy, can be a great help for certain people. It seems to aid in releasing blocked energy for one thing, and acts as a kind of housecleaning.

Q. How would you advise someone who is about to embark on Zen practice?

A. I'd say find a teacher you can trust and begin practicing, following the teacher's directions as precisely as possible. Then check in with the teacher from time to time and sit with a group when you can. For the rest, it's a matter of giving yourself up, of letting go.

Q. So you think it's important to have frequent contact with a teacher?

A. Yes. Not everyone can have as frequent contact as they'd like, but it's important to have someone you can write to and talk with on occasion. The opportunities for self-delusion are so great that most people need to have somebody with whom to check. And people on the Way need encouragement. I heard Thomas Keating say recently that the purpose of the teacher is to give guidance, to encourage, and to be an example by embodying the teaching. That last is the hardest for the teacher to provide, of course.

Q. You spoke of bringing Zen practice into our daily life. How do you recommend we do that?

A. Our practice is to bring us to realize this moment. We have to stop living in our thoughts, to stop wishing for something that's not here or avoiding what is, and to start being in the present. The process of practice is bringing attention to nothing else but the breath or koan, etc., in this moment. Then when we get up from our cushion we carry that same kind of attention over into each moment. Just being here now, life starts to flow. It's important that we don't practice only while we're sitting.

Q. Did you find that you learned this gradually over a long period of time?

A. Yes. It's not easy for me yet. I'm still working on it, but life gets more and more simple.

Q. Many women practicing Zen are beginning families and are finding it difficult to have time to sit, especially when children are very young. Do you have any suggestions on how they should practice?

A. To be every moment right where they are. To be right there, and not wishing they were somewhere else, wishing to be on the cushion, for example. We have to realize that every state of mind is it—that delusion is enlightenment, enlightenment delusion. Taking care of that baby is essentially the same as practice on the cushion, as long as one is right here in the moment. There is nowhere else.

Q. One of the problems within a lay sangha is that people are busy making a living, raising families, keeping up their houses, etc. How much practice do you think a person needs on their cushion?

A. I think we all have to gauge that for ourselves based on our own needs and obligations. As I said, our whole life is our practice. How much time someone is able to sit will vary. Times of intensive practice help greatly, but if your life situation makes that impossible, that's okay, too. There's often a big temptation for persons on the spiritual way to leave their ordinary life behind and seek a greater involvement in "practice," but they have to realize that our practice is always done right where we are. If we surrender to the moment, the next step takes care of itself. I like the Zen caution, "Look under your feet."

Q. At the beginning of this interview we spoke briefly about spiritual experiences. Zazen contributes to having these experiences. How do Zen experiences relate to living in the moment?

A. In kensho, or realization, nothing changes at all, only your awareness. It's like waking up to the moment, to what's right here now.

You realize there is nothing else. Harada Roshi used the analogy of someone being born blind and gradually gaining their sight. The world doesn't change at all. It's just that you become able to see. Kensho may be only a hazy glimpse, but you keep on practicing and you see more. It's a gradual process, over years.

Q. And all this leads to being able to live more fully in the moment?

A. You can't live more fully in each moment. You are living totally in each moment whether you are aware of it or not. Only our awareness or realization changes. Master Bankei says we don't have to do anything at all—just know that the perfect unborn mind is constantly working in all of us. But we can only "know" that with realization. And you can't give that realization to anyone by telling them about it.

Q. Two experiences spoken of frequently are the oneness experience and the experience of emptiness. How do you see these relating to each other and to living right here in the moment?

A. People seem to come fairly easy to the experience of oneness, but without the experience of emptiness we cannot say that it's a real kensho. If there's an experience of emptiness, the realization of oneness is a natural outcome. It is only because it is empty that it is one. This changes a person's perception of reality, as I said, not the fact of reality. In kensho we realize that the present moment is *it*. There is nothing outside of it to strive for, nothing in it to avoid. It's the experience of complete satisfaction with exactly what is happening.

Contributors

ROBERT AITKEN is Executive Director of the Diamond Sangha and Roshi at its centers: The Koko An Zendo and the Maui Zendo in Hawaii, the Sydney Zen Centre and the Zen Group of Western Australia in Australia, the Ring of Bone Zendo in Nevada City, California, and the Zen Desert Sangha in Tucson. He is a Dharma successor of Yamada Koun Roshi, Abbot of the Sanbokyodan school of Zen Buddhism, also known as the Harada-Yasutani line. Aitken Roshi is author of *A Zen Wave: Basho's Haiku and Zen* (Weatherhill), *Taking the Path of Zen* (North Point) and *The Mind of Clover: Essays in Zen Buddhist Ethics* (North Point). Aitken Roshi lives with his wife Anne in Honolulu.

CHARLOTTE JOKO BECK began studying Zen twenty years ago and has practiced with Yasutani Roshi, Soen Roshi and Maezumi Roshi. Currently Joko is teaching at San Diego Zen Center. To her work as a teacher of Zen, Joko brings her varied experiences as a mother and grandmother, pianist, music teacher and businesswoman.

CARLA BRENNAN began Buddhist practice in 1975 and has studied primarily in the Zen and Theravadan traditions. She is a visual artist, working as a painter, illustrator and teacher. Carla currently lives in western Massachusetts.

FLORA COURTOIS has studied Zen since 1950 and is one of the founders of the Zen Center of Los Angeles. She has worked as a public relations director, clinical research psychologist, and university lecturer. Currently she is President-Emeritus of The Foundation for Traditional Studies, which she founded in 1984 in Santa Barbara, California and Washington, D.C.

RITA M. GROSS is a professor in the Department of Philosophy and Religious Studies at the University of Wisconsin, Eau Claire. She has published numerous articles on Buddhism and feminism as well as on other aspects of feminist thought. She is also involved in Buddhist-Christian dialogue.

MICHELE HILL became a member of the Diamond Sangha and the *Kahawai* collective in 1979. She is currently working at the University of Hawaii on a special education research grant. She also teaches adults with developmental disabilities and does volunteer work in the area of sex abuse prevention for children.

DEBORAH HOPKINSON has been practicing Zen since 1975 with Robert Aitken and the Diamond Sangha, and was a co-founder of *Kahawai* in 1979. She received her Master's degree in Asian Studies and is now a Development Director with the University of Hawaii Foundation. She lives in Honolulu with her husband and daughter and continues to be part of the *Kahawai* collective.

EILEEN KIERA began practicing Zen Buddhism in 1980. She recently returned to Washington after spending two years in Hawaii studying with Robert Aitken Roshi. Her home is in the northwestern woods where she works as a biologist and environmentalist.

JOANNA MACY encountered Buddhism in the mid-sixties when she lived in India with her husband and three children. A student of Vipassana, she has studied and become a spokesperson for the Sarvodaya movement in Sri Lanka. Joanna is the author of *Dharma and Development* (Kumarian Press, rev. ed., 1985) and *Despair and Personal Power in the Nuclear Age* (New Society Publishers, 1983). Based on her studies and experience she has developed despair and empowerment workshops which are given in many post-industrial countries.

MICHELE MARTIN currently practices in the world of nine-to-five as an editor at the State University of New York Press and spends the rest of her time at Karma Dharmachakra, a Tibetan Buddhist center in Woodstock, New York.

SUSAN MURCOTT co-founded *Kahawai* with Deborah Hopkinson at the Maui Zendo training period during the winter of 1979. She was an active member of both the *Kahawai* collective and the Diamond Sangha for five years. In 1983 Susan returned to the Boston area where she now teaches meditation and is in the continuing education program at Wellesley College.

JOAN RIECK was born in Manitowoc, Wisconsin in 1936. She lived in Japan for 18 years and first came in contact with Zen there in the mid-sixties. In 1972 she began studying with Yamada Roshi in Kamakura and received permission to teach in 1983. She currently teaches Zen to groups in Lucerne, Switzerland and in Seattle, Washington.

SUSAN SUNTREE writes, performs and lives with her family in Santa Monica, California. Her studies of ritual and origins of art influence her work which includes a cycle of seasonal plays, *Seed to Snow—Plays for the Seasons*, two books of poetry, *Eye of the Womb* and *Bold Friends*, and a one-woman ritual performance, *Origins of Praise*. She is a consultant in arts for the disabled, a teacher, and has a lifelong interest in women's and environmental issues.

FRAN TRIBE began her Zen practice at Berkeley Zendo in 1967 and was a student of Suzuki Roshi before his death. She has also practiced at Tassajara and at Koko An Zendo in Honolulu. Fran lives in Berkeley with her husband and two children and recently served as president of the Berkeley Zen Center.

TERESA VAST grew up in California but has lived and practiced with the Diamond Sangha in Hawaii for the past 13 years. Her article, "Parent-birth," was written shortly after the birth of her daughter, Angela, in February, 1982. Teresa is currently Director of Children's Programs with the YWCA of Oahu.

MARGOT WALLACH MILLIKEN began practicing Buddhist meditation in 1974. From 1977 to 1980 she lived in Hawaii where she was a student of Aitken Roshi and a founding member of the *Kahawai* collective. She now lives in Cumberland, Maine with her husband and son.

JUDITH WRIGHT was born in 1915 in New South Wales, Australia and is a longtime conservation activist and author. She has published twelve books of poetry including *The Double Tree* (Houghton Mifflin) and has also written a number of books of prose including essays and books for children.

Glossary

bodhisattva	(Sanskrit) one on the path to enlightenment; one who is enlightened; one who enlightens others.
Buddha	(Sanskrit) enlightened one; Shakyamuni; one of several figures in the Buddhist pantheon.
Dharma	(Sanskrit) law: religious, secular, natural; the law of Karma; affinity, phenomena; Tao or Way; a teaching; the void.
dokusan	(Japanese) sanzen; to go or work alone; personal interview with the roshi.
gassho	(Japanese) hands palm-to-palm in a spirit of respect or devotion.
Kanzeon	(Japanese) Kannon; Avalokiteshvara; the One Who Perceives the Sounds of the World; incarnation of mercy and compassion.
kensho	(Japanese) to see nature; to see into essential nature; gnostic experience in Zen practice.
koan	(Japanese) a theme of zazen to be made clear; an expression of harmony of empty oneness with the world of particulars; a story or saying handed down in the Buddhist tradition.
Mahayana	(Sanskrit) Great Vehicle; the northern Buddhism of China, Korea and Japan (Vajrayana, or Tibetan Buddhism, is often included in this classification).
mu	(Japanese) Wu; No; does not have; First case of the *Mumonkan*, a collection of koans (Mu is often the first koan of the Zen student).

nirvana	(Sanskrit) extinction of craving; the wisdom presented in the world of particulars.
Rinzai	(Japanese) the Rinzai Zen Buddhist school, traced from Lin-chi, ninth century.
roshi	(Japanese) venerable teacher.
samadhi	(Sanskrit) concentration; the quality of meditation.
sangha	(Sanskrit) Buddhist fellowship; fellowship; harmony of Buddha and Dharma.
sesshin	(Japanese) to touch, receive or convey the mind; the Zen retreat, conventionally seven days.
shikantaza	(Japanese) breath watching; just sitting.
Soto	(Japanese) the Soto Zen Buddhist school, traced from Tung-shan Liang-chieh, ninth century.
sutra	(Sanskrit) sermons attributed to the Buddha; Buddhist scriptures.
Tao	(Chinese) Bodhi or enlightenment; Way; the way of enlightenment.
teisho	(Japanese) presentation of the call; the roshi's Dharma talk.
zazen	(Japanese) seated meditation; Zen meditation.
Zen	(Japanese) Ch'an; the Zen Buddhist sect; the harmony of empty oneness and the world of particulars.
zendo	(Japanese) meditation hall.

Members of the *Kahawai* collective at Koko An Zendo in Honolulu.